THERE'S
SOMETHING
UNDER
the BED!

THERE'S SOMETHING UNDER THE BED!

Children's Experiences With the Paranormal

BY URSULA BIELSKI

Foreword by Jeff Belanger

New Page BOOKS

A division of The Career Press, Inc.
Pompton Plains, NJ

THERE'S SOMETHING UNDER THE BED
Edited by Nicole DeFelice
Typeset by Diana Ghazzawi
Cover art by Ian Daniels
Printed in the U.S.A. by Courier

To order this title, please call toll-free 1-800-CAREER-1 (NJ and Canada: 201-848-0310) to order using VISA or MasterCard, or for further information on books from Career Press.

The Career Press, Inc.
220 West Parkway, Unit 12
Pompton Plains, NJ 07444
www.careerpress.com
www.newpagebooks.com

Library of Congress Cataloging-in-Publication Data

CIP data available upon request.

For D, who knows the monsters are real.

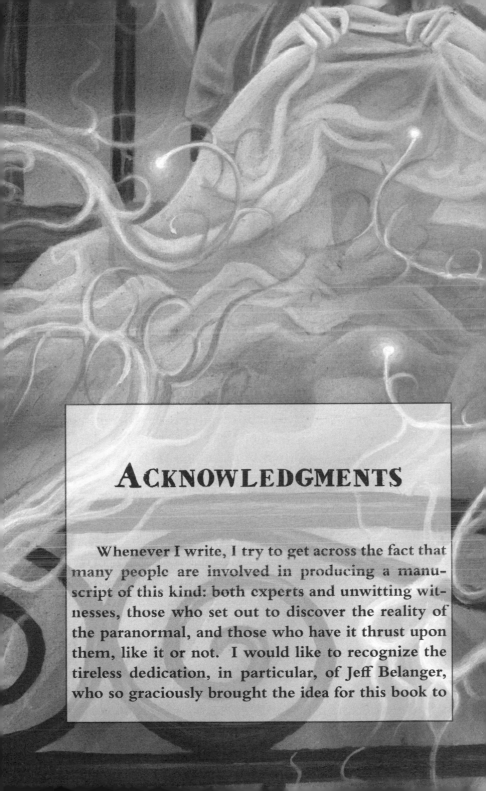

ACKNOWLEDGMENTS

Whenever I write, I try to get across the fact that many people are involved in producing a manuscript of this kind: both experts and unwitting witnesses, those who set out to discover the reality of the paranormal, and those who have it thrust upon them, like it or not. I would like to recognize the tireless dedication, in particular, of Jeff Belanger, who so graciously brought the idea for this book to the attention of Michael Pye at New Page Books, and who has spent each and every day for more than 10 years giving a voice to paranormal experiencers at GhostVillage.com, filling the bookshelves of ghost hunters around the world, and providing endless encouragement and support to people like me. He is the greatest cheerleader and friend anyone could have, and I am honored that he accepted the invitation to write the foreword for this volume.

I want to thank Michael Pye for giving me the chance to write this book and editor Kirsten Dalley for her patient and knowledgeable direction in the completion of it. Many thanks, too, to my research assistant, Cynthia Pelayo, who dug up a lot of interesting notes to get me started on some of my more daunting topics.

Many thanks to those who provided their own experiences, especially those who contributed verbatim accounts, including Trish Baldwin, David Schnoebelen, and particularly, David Slone of TrueGhostTales.com, who kindly granted permission to reproduce accounts from his ever-growing collection of readers' true stories. Thanks to Kathleen Erickson of the *Journal for Scientific Exploration* for permission to share the late Ian Stevenson's information and photographs on birthmarks relating to past lives of children; I hope readers will find their skepticism on the subject as challenged as mine was when confronted with Dr. Stevenson's amazing findings.

Many thanks to Lorraine Warren who, along with her late husband, Ed, has contributed so much to the field of paranormal research. In addition to being one of the world's greatest investigators, she is just such a kind person.

The chilling story of Annabelle the Doll was a must-have for this book, and I'm grateful for the opportunity to share it.

At home, on a very practical level, I am continuously grateful to the Chicago Public Library for always guiding me when I'm not sure where I need to go. The staff of its many branches has been with me throughout my writing career, and I'm so fortunate to have access to such a valuable—and personally helpful—resource.

Thank you, David, for taking care of the girls every day, so I could write, and for running the business end of things so I could concentrate. And thank you, Eva and Ilse, for being so proud of me all the time, no matter how strange I may appear to others!

Finally, I'm very grateful to all of those who have supported my writing and research all these years. All of my friends and colleagues; all the bleary-eyed ghost hunters who are out there all night, freezing and often frustrated, looking patiently for the needles in the paranormal haystack; all who enthusiastically and trustingly share their experiences year after year. I promise I'll never stop telling your stories.

From ghoulies and ghosties
Long-leggedy beasties
And things that go bump in the night…
Good Lord, deliver us.

—Old Scottish prayer

Contents

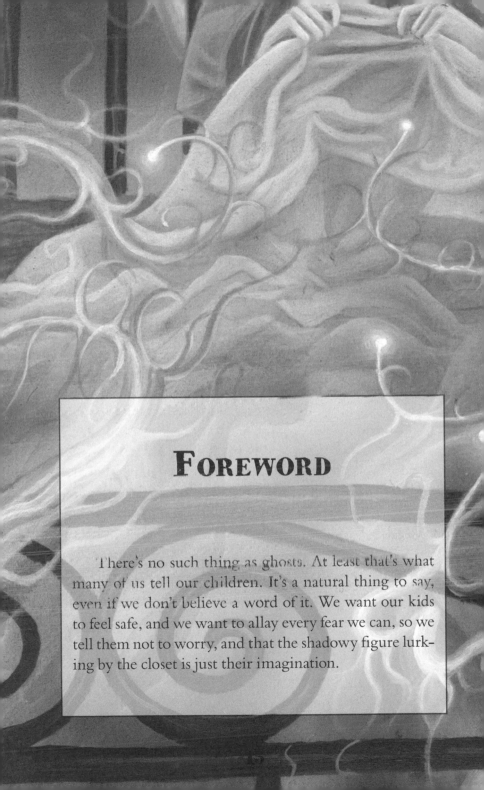

FOREWORD

There's no such thing as ghosts. At least that's what many of us tell our children. It's a natural thing to say, even if we don't believe a word of it. We want our kids to feel safe, and we want to allay every fear we can, so we tell them not to worry, and that the shadowy figure lurking by the closet is just their imagination.

Likewise, when children tell us of their "invisible" friends, we parents tell ourselves this is just a flight of fancy for our offspring. We want to feel safe, too. We may love to discuss ghosts and haunted places, but we'd prefer they not necessarily live with us, thank you very much.

We live during a time of unprecedented paranormal discussion. All forms of media inundate us with content about ghosts, demons, monsters, and other unexplained phenomena. These subjects are going to filter down to our children; we can't stop it. And our children are going to have questions, because all children want to figure out the world around them. Of course we must assure our children that they're safe, but there's so much they can tell us about the world they see and experience.

The paranormal isn't just for adults anymore. Not that it ever was. I recall my interest in the subject being born out of a Ouija board session around age 10 during a sleepover at a friend's old haunted home. My intrigue gave way to further questions, my questions led me to reading all the books I could find, the reading led me to investigations, and somewhere along the way I realized my thirst for the unexplained would never be quenched. Now that I'm a dad, I can think of worse paths for my own child.

I recall my daughter, Sophie, at 14 months old, sitting in the living room of my *not*-haunted house. She was sitting and playing when something caught her attention over my wife's shoulder. She gave a big grin and waved. The only thing over my wife's shoulder was an empty corner of the room. My daughter had done nothing like that before or since. She only knows she saw something that seemed friendly, so she smiled and waved—just as she would to someone smiling at her in the grocery store.

As my daughter grows, she's starting to ask questions about what her daddy does for a living. The words *ghosts* and *paranormal* are thrown around my home quite a bit. As a paranormal researcher, I want to tell her everything—all of the theories, what I believe, and what I've seen. As her daddy, I don't want her to be scared. As of this writing, she's 3 years old. She likes to throw a blanket over her head and say, "I'm a ghost...oooooooo!" She talks about ghosts in the same manner she talks about butterflies or dogs. We don't go on and on about the subject, but when it comes up, I'm happy to let her lead the discussion. I have no doubt that a paranormal guy like me can learn a lot from a 3-year-old. Sophie often speaks whatever she is thinking about. There's no filter, so I get to hear all of it. If she starts talking to someone I can't see or if she describes conversations, I will give her my full attention. If it's only her imagination, I won't discourage her. I want her to have a wonderful imagination. If it's something more, I still won't discourage her. I'll listen. I want her to know she can talk about these subjects with me.

As parents, we need to decide what role (if any) organized religion is going to play in the lives of our families, and we need to decide how much of our own interest in the paranormal we want to incorporate into this spiritual discussion.

There's no point in telling our children that the paranormal is dangerous and should be avoided. I can think of no better way to make an already-fascinating subject even more alluring. We can't hide from ghosts, but we can use this topic as an opportunity.

Ghosts are an innovative way to teach history to our children. Facts, figures, dates, and names are cold and have little meaning. To tell a middle-schooler that more than 800 people were killed during the First Battle of Bull Run on July 21, 1861, doesn't say much. But to tell a child there's a ghost lurking the woods near Manassas, Virginia, and people think his name is Billy, a soldier who fought and died here, a man who is still looking for his comrades because of his eternal sense of duty, a man who left behind a crying wife and child, well…now we have a story. History is the stage we set for our ghosts. Understand just one ghost's story at Bull Run, and then a child can multiply that by 800 and get a sense of what the sacrifices really mean.

Today there are families who ghost hunt together, and who explore the unexplained as a family unit. What a unique vacation idea! These folks are legend tripping, working to-gether, learning history, and forming a bond that cannot be matched by throwing skee ball at some boardwalk arcade.

To discuss ghosts is a safe way to explore the notion of death and mortality. Children as young as 2 years old start to learn the concept of death. It's an important lesson because everything dies. Ghosts offer a more comfortable way to broach the topic before the hard lesson of Grandma passing on makes it too emotionally charged and difficult. Ghosts also offer kids hope that we won't be forgotten after we die, and there's your segue into your religious belief system. Religion is complex. Ghosts can be remarkably easy.

Children are more sensitive to the world than adults. They're smarter than most give them credit for. Children can sense and react to the emotions of their parents long before they can walk or talk. Why are children so sensitive? Survival. They can't fight or run, but they can cry for help. If they see something they fear, they cry. If they see something they like, they coo and smile. Young children may be the world's most perfectly tuned spirit detector (not that I'm advocating using children as ghost bait...but then again... hmmm).

What you're holding in your hands is a great addition to the discussion of the paranormal and children. From the creatures once held only in the realm of fairytales, to the clinical study of psychic phenomenon, there is much to discuss and learn from *There's Something Under the Bed*. To experience the world through a child's eyes is one of the greatest joys of parenthood. That world, by the way, includes the world of the supernatural. We owe it to our kids and to ourselves to bring these subjects to the forefront, because through understanding we can minimize fear and foster a sense of wonder and learning.

I'd like to thank Ursula Bielski both as a parent and as a paranormal researcher for shedding such credible light on this important paranormal topic.

—Jeff Belanger
Founder of *Ghostvillage.com*,
host of *30 Odd Minutes*,
and author of *The World's Most Haunted Places*
and *Who's Haunting the White House?*

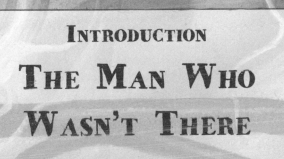

INTRODUCTION

THE MAN WHO
WASN'T THERE

When I was growing up in Chicago, my life was filled with paranormal happenings, stories, and experiences of my own and of my family—some of them passed down through generations. Like many children, I lived in a confounding world where adults would thrill us during the day with stories of apparitions, visions, and ghostly visitations, only to tell us at bedtime that "there are no such things."

Every neighborhood has a haunted house, and the year before I was born my parents bought the haunted house in the area where my mom had grown up, not far from Wrigley Field. Though my parents were both rational, they were not strangers to the paranormal. My mom often told of how her parents woke together one night during World War II to see their son, Will, standing at the foot of their bed and then vanishing into thin air. Will had been serving overseas in Japan and, predictably, his family received a telegram the next day informing them of his death on Saipan—at the moment they'd seen him in their room. My dad was a police officer, and calls often came in from terrified citizens reporting "intruders"—footsteps, slamming doors, voices—though nothing and no one would be found by police. As a child, he'd had many experiences of the paranormal, including the chilling afternoon when he says he saw the tail of the Devil himself—red and pointed—hanging out of a window of his boyhood home.

Our own home turned out to be more haunted than my parents were at first willing to acknowledge. The very first night—while they were still renovating—they heard footsteps in the uninhabitable upstairs hall. The first night they slept upstairs, they heard the unmistakable sound of footfalls on the stairs. The very first memory I recall is of waking up in my crib to the sound of these phantom footfalls, an experience that was repeated every night for 12 years, until they seemed to fade away, never to return. I am sure she meant to alleviate our fears, but my mom's insistence that the footsteps weren't real caused much more real fear than the idea that they were genuine. Our fear went on, night after night, year after year. We lived and slept with a ghost in the house, but we were not allowed to believe it was there. Curiously, my dad took the opposite approach. "It's spooks," he used to say. "Go back to sleep."

THEY'RE EVERYWHERE

When my brother, my cousins, and I were children, what the adults didn't realize was that we were afraid almost everywhere we went. Each family's house, it seemed, had its own dreadful stories and events, and even when we went on trips, we'd have to pass the huge cemeteries on Irving Park Road or Addison Street, our eyes tightly shut.

A few blocks away, at my Uncle Gene's house, my Aunt Katie told of her weekly run-ins with the ghost of the previous owner, who had hanged himself in the garage the winter before she and my uncle bought the house. Each Wednesday night, when he'd go out to his lodge meeting, she would hear a rattle in the kitchen and watch the doorknob turn, as if the erstwhile owner were coming in from his death site for an invisible nightcap.

My maternal grandma's house, where cousins and I would sleep over in the summertime, was believed to be haunted by her first child, baby Frances, who had died of pneumonia around 1920. The bedroom where she died was haunted by the sound of a baby crying, from the time of the death up through my childhood in the 1970s. My Uncle Joe slept lived in my grandma's attic his whole life, and for years after after he died—after a heart attack on the couch—we would hear his old barbells rolling across the attic floor at night.

It wasn't long before I discovered that these phenomena were not always personal but sometimes reached out to fascinate whole neighborhoods, parishes, sometimes even the whole city, and that they often endure as communal ghost stories, urban legends, and other tales that—like family stories of the paranormal—are passed down through generations. A favorite place for me—in the daytime—was nearby Graceland Cemetery, the final resting place to some of Chicago's most important architects, merchants, and settlers. As a child my dad would take me there to teach me about Chicago history, but I was more interested in catching a glimpse of little Inez Clarke, a tiny ghost girl said to haunt the statue over her grave.

EXTRAORDINARY EXPERIENCES

I knew from the stories my parents, aunts, uncles, and grandparents told that experiences of the paranormal were not exclusive to us. They are common through the generations, and these experiences have a tremendous impact on children's lives. In fact, one of my earliest conscious observations was realizing how childhood experiences of the paranormal deeply affected my parents, aunts, and uncles even decades after they occurred. Unfortunately, I was learning at the same time that these experiences are extraordinary, and I was taught that extraordinary experiences are not a desirable part of normal life.

The ghosts I already knew came from awful, real events: the insanity of our home's previous owner, the suicide of the owner of my uncle's home, the death of a baby at Grandma's, many years before, and the death of Inez Clarke, a tuberculosis victim of just 4 years old.

However, when I grew up and began to study the paranormal, I began to realize that, though I'd had my own terrifying experiences with ghosts, as many children do, only the smallest portion of children's paranormal experiences are recognized by themselves or the adults in their lives. This is because children live in a liminal or transitional space where they don't notice the presence of the paranormal as paranormal. They haven't learned to shut these experiences out, and because most of the experiences are not frightening in and of themselves, they do not cause concern.

LIMINALITY AND THE PARANORMAL

Parapsychologist George Hansen wrote much about the connection between liminal states and the experiencing of the paranormal. In particular, in his essay, "Ghosts and Liminality," he points out:

> Liminality applies to change, transition, and transformation—conditions that are conducive to psi phenomena. For instance, poltergeist effects tend to occur around someone in puberty. A person at that stage in life is neither a child nor an adult, but rather is betwixt and between those roles.

Psi is the term parapsychologists use to generically refer to all kinds of psychic phenomena, experiences, or events that seem to be related to the psyche or mind, and which cannot be explained by established physical principles.

This "in between" stage of liminality leaves the individual in a world where neither the consciousness of infancy (an awareness that adults do not have) nor of adulthood are present. There is, instead, a freedom from both, where many things may be perceived, understood, and possibly even affected by the transitional person.

Adults tend to dismiss all paranormal experiences as "imagination." They may not be far off, if we're willing to rethink what we mean by the word. Again, children live in that liminal world where they do not have blocks up in their mind against these phenomena. So, to adults, that "imagination", that willingness to see beyond what is "real," or possible, may be an ability to live in a world where children see all that really is there, not just what adults have been conditioned to accept as "reality."

1

BIRTH OF THE BOOGEYMAN

Ignoring the possible paranormal nature of children's experiences is really both unfair and ineffective, especially since so much of the "innocent" children's culture that we want them to experience is rife with paranormal events and possibilities. It's also the place where we inadvertently teach children to negatively view the paranormal, and to fear it.

Witches have endured generations of negative press, thanks to stories like *Cinderella*, *Snow White*, and *Hansel and Gretel*. And while good witches do join the bad, they pale in reputation and in physical description beside the dark and malicious "bad witches" of children's tales. From earliest childhood, ghosts are identified to children as entities that either don't exist or don't belong among the living. We discourage invisible friends, believing them to be unreal, and we look upon the interest in death, cemeteries, and the spirits as morbid tendencies.

Very important to remember is that, while teaching our children to be *unafraid* in their beds at home, as "there's nothing in the closet, nothing under the bed," we at once unwittingly teach them that, at any moment, otherworldly figures are not only watching them, but have the ability to come into the home—into their very rooms—to confront them at any time. Often, these unnerving lessons come to them through folktales and written literature.

When my brother and I were children, growing up partly among my mom's family of German descent, we were often disciplined—as many are—with warnings from our ethnic folklore. A frightening fixture at my maternal grandmother's house was a book called *Struwwelpeter* or *Shock-headed Peter*. The book, by German author Heinrich Hoffman, presents 10 illustrated, rhyming stories, each of them teaching a moral lesson. Almost every story deals with the awful, and sometimes deadly, consequences of childhood misbehavior.

In "Die gar traurige Geschichte mit dem Feuerzeug" ("The Very Sad Story of the Matches"), a girl plays with matches and burns to death. In "Die Geschichte vom

Suppen-Kaspar" ("The Story of Kaspar's Soup"), a healthy little boy named Kaspar decides to stop eating his dinner. During the course of a few days he wastes away and dies. In "Die Geschichte vom fliegenden Robert" ("The Story of Flying Robert"), a boy foolishly takes a walk during a storm. The wind gets under his umbrella and carries him away forever.

Without question, the most horrifying story in the book is that of "Die Geschichte vom Daumenlutscher" ("The Story of Thumb-Sucker"). In it, a mother scolds her son for sucking his thumbs. He behaves until she leaves the house, when he immediately resumes his thumb sucking. Shockingly, a mysterious tailor appears in the house and cuts off the boy's thumbs with giant scissors. When we were children, the idea of this stranger knowing our actions and appearing in the house with malicious intent was an appalling one. Clearly, the tailor was possessed of otherworldly powers, as he was not only aware of children's naughty deeds but able to appear in their homes and attack them.

The dreaded Tailor of *Der Struwwelpeter,* the stuff of German children's nightmares. *(Photograph from* Der Struwwelpeter *by Heinrich Hoffman, originally published in 1845.)*

Another such character from German lore was that

of "Der Sandmann" ("The Sandman"). American culture paints a sweet and cozy portrait of this nocturnal visitor: a nightcapped gentleman who sprinkles sand in the eyes of children who are still awake when he arrives in their rooms. According to this tame version of the tale, the sand helps lull children to sleep and good dreams, and the "sleep" in one's eyes upon waking is evidence of the Sandman's work. Far from a frightening figure, this Sandman is benign and full of good wishes for children.

The German "Sandmann" was a much more sinister creature. In the novel *Der Sandmann* by E.T.A. Hoffman, the nursemaid describes him as

> [a] wicked man, who comes to children when they won't go to bed, and throws a handful of sand into their eyes, so that they start out bleeding from their heads. He puts their eyes in a bag and carries them to the crescent moon to feed his own children, who sit in the nest up there. They have crooked beaks like owls so that they can pick up the eyes of naughty human children.

In the song "Enter Sandman," the rock band Metallica perfectly captures not only the personality of the malevolent Sandmann, but what children truly feel when they face bedtime in a home where unknown terrors really do lurk after lights out.

The benevolent character of Santa Claus is one treasured by children, and his paranormal ability to see our children when they're sleeping and to know if they have been bad or good is a helpful tool in disciplining children who are counting on Christmas toys. Still, when Christmas comes, there is a good amount of fear that appears in children. Despite their wishes for gifts, there is something distinctly unsettling about the idea of a person who knows your thoughts and actions coming into your home in the middle of the night by unknown means. It's not surprising, however, that Santa Claus has these incredible abilities, because his prototype, Saint Nicholas, had some of his own.

St. Nicholas and the restored children, from *La Legende de Saint Nicolas,* original French edition, illustrated by A. Boursier-Mougenot, 1935. *(StNicholasCenter.org.)*

Before canonizing (bestowing sainthood upon) one of the faithful, the Catholic Church requires proof that the person performed at least one miracle, and Nicholas performed a number of them. However, the story of one such miracle is a deeply disturbing one.

The story tells of three young seminarians who stop at an inn on their way to attend school in Athens. According to accounts, the innkeeper robbed them of their money, sold their horses, and murdered the young men, hiding their remains in a large pickle barrel. Bishop Nicholas, traveling through the same countryside, had also stopped at the inn

Black Peter, St. Nicholas' diabolical sidekick, terrorizes a child on Christmas morning.

and, during the night, he had a dream about the crime, got up from his bed, and found the boys' gruesome remains. Nicholas prayed fervently for God to save the students, and their bodies were miraculously restored to life and wholeness. This is why every German Christmas tree includes a glass ornament in the shape of a pickle.

In France the story tells of three little children who wander away from home while playing, and who fall into the hands of a demented butcher who dismembers them and attempts to pickle the parts for later sale. Again, Nicholas is said to have had a vision of the atrocious crime and to have successfully prayed for restoration of the children's bodies.

American children are accustomed to the image of Santa Claus attended by friendly, childlike elves, but European tradition portrays a much different sort of helper. Nicholas's assistant is an evil, dark-faced character known as "Black Peter," once believed to be the Devil himself, who is forced to serve St. Nicholas on his gift-giving rounds. According to legend, Black Peter is responsible for leaving switches or rods as punishment to naughty children, while Nicholas is privileged to leave the candy and toys. It's not surprising, then, that European children fear as much as anticipate the arrival of Christmas each year.

From earliest infancy, we instill children with an awareness of paranormal powers and figures. Though the best intentions motivate us, sometimes the frightening aspects of children's stories—and the powers of the characters that populate them—can instill a very early fear of the paranormal. Whether we invoke Santa Claus's psychic abilities when threatening our children to behave—or pass down ancient tales of bad witches and other creatures of the night, a wise parent will keep in mind that children are building their consciousness all the time. It's up to us to realize that a consciousness of the paranormal doesn't have to begin in fear.

2
CLAIRVOYANCE OF FAIRIES

As adults, we assume that children live in a world where reality and imagination hold equal sway, but this may not be as true as we think. Many paranormal researchers believe that much of what we pass off as imaginary in children may actually be part of a reality of which most adults are not aware. Sometimes, children may truly see things adults don't.

The paranormal gift of seeing what others don't is called clairvoyance. It is a real gift, but, though few adults can claim it, we all seem to own it for a little while from birth, for an unspecified amount of time. It begins when we start to realize that certain experiences are "unacceptable" to adults, while certain realities do "fit" into adult perceptions. The age varies, depending on how early the child is exposed to rejection of the paranormal. Over the centuries, no brand of clairvoyance has been more closely associated with children than the seeing of and interaction with fairies.

When my young daughters and I first moved into our flat on Chicago's north side, not far from Wrigley Field, they began what would become a ritual of going out into the front garden each evening to "feed the fairies." They built chairs and a table of twigs, which they placed in the dirt under the evergreen shrubs, lent their tiny tea set for the fairies' use, and offered bits of cookies, raisins, and diminutive bowls of milk and lemonade. We have been here for almost three years now, and my daughters still leave their gifts and search for the fairies at summer twilights. Sometimes I hear them talking to them, and I smile, but I wonder if it is imagination at play.

In 1922, the great Scottish writer Sir Arthur Conan Doyle completed a divisive volume entitled *The Coming of the Fairies*, based on his two years of involvement in the controversial world of the so-called Cottingley Fairies. The alleged fairies were "captured" on a still-debated series of photographs taken by two young girls outside their home in

Cottingley, England, which depicted what appeared to be fairies and even a gnome frolicking with the children.

Generations later, Elsie Wright and Frances Griffiths, cousins, publicly admitted to faking the photographs using cardboard cutouts. Still, they forever held that they had created the hoax to prove the existence of the very real fairies in their garden to non-believing adults, particularly Elsie's mother and father, with whom the girls were living. Frances maintained until her death that the fifth photograph in the series—which depicted a gathering of fairies, but neither of the girls—was genuine.

Cousins Frances Griffiths and Elsie Wright convinced some of the greatest minds of their day that there were fairies living in their garden in Cottingley, England. *(Wikipedia.)*

The photographs first came to Conan Doyle's attention via Edward Gardner, a well-known Theosophist, who received the prints from Polly Wright, Elsie's mother, who at the time was developing an interest in theosophy and other spiritual ideas. Though Gardner believed the photographs were authentic, Sir Oliver Lodge, one of the first practitioners of psychical research, pronounced at once that the prints— and the girls—were frauds. Conan Doyle, however, was a practicing spiritualist, having come to the religion after the closely occurring deaths of his wife, his son, his brother, his two brothers-in-law, and his two nephews. Eager to discover the truth behind the prints, Conan Doyle asked Gardner to go to Cottingley to meet with Elsie and Frances, and to try to persuade the girls to take more photographs. Gardner found the girls believable and the family stable, and he left with the girls' two new cameras and a stack of photographic plates, along with his rousing encouragement.

When new photos resulted, Gardner sent them on to Conan Doyle, then on a pro-Spiritualist lecture tour in Australia, who saw the fresh prints as the imminent "visible sign" of the spiritual world that had been promised by spirits in recent séances he had attended.

Previously, Conan Doyle had published a selection of the initial photographs in an article for the Christmas issue of the wildly popular English magazine *The Strand*, which sold out within days. Controversy over the article had rocked the nation, opinion split fiercely between wide-eyed wonder and sheer disgust. But while Conan Doyle hoped the new photos would convince both the fence sitters and stalwart skeptics, he found himself the center of much of the lingering controversy instead: How could this brilliant man be taken in by the obviously deceitful antics of two country girls?

The famous final photograph. Until her death, Frances Griffiths maintained that this photo was genuine. *(Wikipedia.)*

Much of the criticism of Conan Doyle that remains to this day can likely be credited to the public editions of the photographs themselves, as theorized by writer Barbara Roden. Roden suggests that the retouched images that were first printed (and continue to be) appear gravely fraudulent to modern critics, though the originals were much less sharp, the subjects much less defined and "flat" (one of the primary public criticisms over time). The original photographs were sold at auction in 1998 as part of Frances', collection for more than 21,000 pounds and appeared on a Belfast-based edition of *Antiques Roadshow* in 2009, along with the camera that had been given to Frances by Conan Doyle. Frances', daughter also appeared on the show and talked about her mother's embarrassment over her deceit, as well as her mother's insistence that the fifth photo was real. As Roden writes, under the modern lens the case against Doyle emerges—like the photographs themselves—as "less clear-cut than critics would have us believe."

WHAT ARE THEY?

Fairies have held a central place in children's imaginations for centuries, but they were once a central part of the adult world as well. Over the ages, many theories have emerged claiming to identify what they are, exactly.

Some believe that fairies are the spirits of the dead, but those that for some reason and by some mechanism are able to travel between the physical world and the spiritual realm. Another theory holds that fairies are fallen angels, consigned to the earth, cut off from Paradise. Some versions of this theory are tied into an ancient belief that, when the angelic revolution occurred, God ordered the gates of Heaven shut. The angels who were in Heaven at the time remained angels; those who were mixing with the earth became demons, and those in between were consigned to spend eternity as fairies.

This theory would explain the disturbing dual personality of fairies. On the one hand, they are pictured as benevolent nature-lovers, caring for farm animals and the environment, friends to children, even prone to help with housework and farm work. On the other hand, fairies are more traditionally believed to be quite malicious. For centuries they were known for harming those who stood in the way of their activities or who did not give them gifts, typically indulgent foods. They regularly abducted or killed babies, misled travelers, burned barns, poisoned livestock, and drowned those who wronged them. Staying out of their paths and living grounds was the preventive antidote to their ill will. Stories even tell of houses being built with the front and back doors lined up over known fairy paths. These doors were left open at night no matter the weather, so that the fairies would be able to use their usual path without interruption.

In the late 1600s a Scottish native named Robert Kirk attempted to document the culture of his local fairy population in Aberfoyle. His illustrative book was published in 1691, and the *Secret Commonwealth of Elves, Fauns, and Fairies* laid out his findings to the world. Though Kirk's tomb may be found in Aberfoyle today, locals swear all is not as it seems. According to legend, his soul was abducted by fairies after he published his research, as he crossed a known fairy hill in the region. Reports claim that his body was left behind, appearing to be dead. After the burial, Kirk was said to have appeared in a dream of a close friend or relative, claiming that he was imprisoned in "Fairyland" and begging for help in his release. The tale tells that the relation was too scared to follow Kirk's instructions, and that Kirk remains in Fairyland to this day.

Even in modern-day England, these curious tales persist. English native Janet Bord's *A Traveller's Guide to Fairy Sites* was published as recently as 2004; the volume has proved a very popular resource for those drawn to these mystical locales. Along with all of the expected legends, Bord shares some unnerving tales from several counties, including Yorkshire, home to the village of Cottingley. In the late 1980s, during

construction of a new highway—the Stocksbridge bypass—
reports were rife of so-called ghosts at Pearoyd Bridge.
During these months, two security guards driving near the
new road saw a group of very small children playing at the
construction site just after midnight. After driving past them
and realizing the oddity of the situation, they stopped the
car and walked back to find out why they were there at that
hour. No one was to be found, and nary a footprint could be
located, despite the ample muddiness of the area where the
children had been seen. In the days that followed, the workers talked to construction workers at the road who admitted to hearing children singing each night in the same area,
singing that would begin around 11 pm and last into the wee
hours.

Many locals came to believe that these visual and audio
"apparitions" were not of ghosts at all, but of real fairies.
Much like ghosts, fairies are known to become more active
during times when their turf is disturbed—during the reno-
vation of a house, for example, or—in this case—the full-
scale eradication of their natural lair. The difference between
the two situations is significant: Ghosts may try to foil the
project in some way—pulling up the new floorboards or
breaking the new lights—or may simply appear more often,
as if they are keeping an eye on the work's progress. Fairies,
however, are not so lenient. As mentioned, they are most
known for their vindictiveness in the face of mistreatment
and disrespect. Maiming, cursing, and even killing are not
unusual punishments in the eyes of fairies.

One wonders what fates befell the construction workers
of the Stocksbridge bypass.

FAIRIES IN 21ST-CENTURY AMERICA

One of the most unsettling and thought-provoking nights of my long career of ghost hunting fell on a winter's night in the late 1990s, at a farm in northwest Indiana. I always call it "the first night I believed in fairies."

The farm's owner is a woman known simply as Luann. Hundreds of ghost hunters have visited her property over many years, and over those years "Luann's Farm" has become a point of pilgrimage for believers and skeptics alike, from every walk of life. Luann first began to wonder about her property when she moved in and the animals in the barn seemed "spooked" by something that Luann herself couldn't see.

A visit by a clairvoyant brought Luann two pieces of astonishing news.

First, the property where Luann's barn stands is reportedly the site of a so-called "portal," a doorway between the physical and spiritual worlds, that had been opened by Native Americans during the time of Anglo settlement. According to Native American lore, many such portals were opened during the early and mid-19th century, specifically to frustrate and terrify the white encroachers on Native American land, as tradition states that ghosts, demons, and other disembodied entities must enter and exit the physical world via a portal that has been opened for this purpose.

Those living or working in portal areas are, according to sensitives, relentlessly surrounded by otherworldly creatures, which are also known to congregate at portal entrances, much the way the humans loiter at bus, plane, or train terminals. Adding to the inconvenience and unease at such sites is the additional belief that beings coming in through portals tend to attach themselves to living, physical bodies, in order to stabilize themselves and travel more easily. Children or weak-willed adults, it is said, are most prone to these attachments.

As astonishing as this news was for Luann, nothing could prepare her for the clairvoyant's second pronunciation: "You have fairies on your property."

Shocked and disbelieving, Luann listened as her visitor, equally amazed, told her some facts about fairies: that they are extremely rare in North America, that they tend to congregate at portals in natural settings, and that those who have them living on their land are highly fortunate, as they bring good luck if you treat them well. Luann naturally asked what she should do to please her fairies, and the clairvoyant said, "You have to feed them." Of course Luann asked, "What should I feed them?" Her visitor told her that she had to experiment to see what they liked.

So Luann began the bizarre ritual of placing petri dishes of various foods and drinks in the barn and on the hill behind it to see what would go missing in the night. Oddly, foods one might expect to be eaten by animals remained each morning: bits of leftover meat—cooked and raw— vegetables, milk, apples. What disappeared, finally, night after night, was what tradition could have dictated.

Fairies, again, are indulgent creatures. They live well and treat well, and when they are displeased, they punish well. Each morning Luann found only three things consistently gone: her tiny servings of fudge brownies, Jameson Irish whiskey, and Starbucks Frappuccino.

Regularly sated with such luxuries, it seems the fairies have remained. They've given two varieties of evidence: good health, good fortune, and other benefits to Luann herself—and another sort of evidence that has confounded literally hundreds of visiting paranormal researchers. I witnessed it myself.

When I visited Luann's farm, I was taken into the barn along with about 20 other ghost hunters, as I was the guest that evening of a local ghost hunting club, whose meetings always took them to a haunted area site. Most of the others present had brought digital cameras, and they snapped many photographs as we entered the barn and made our way upstairs to the hayloft where the portal has been pinpointed.

Now, "orbs" have been a subject of great controversy in ghost hunting circles over the years. These semi-transparent balls of white light that show up in photographs are believed by some to be balls of spirit energy, and by others to be dust, moisture, or other explicable culprits. With more than twenty people walking into a hay-filled barn, one might well expect orbs to show up on film as the dust is disturbed by all of those footsteps. However, in Luann's barn, nearly 20 cameras caught only a handful of them when we entered.

We settled down and either stood or sat. When we were all quiet and unmoving, Luann began to speak to the fairies.

"Don't be afraid," she said. "No one is here to hurt you, only to learn about you."

She introduced me, as I had never been there before, and as she spoke the blackness was lit, again and again, by the flashes of the cameras going off, dozens of flashes a minute, as the others gathered snapped photo after photo. Luann asked the fairies to come to me, to come and meet me, and, again, to not be afraid.

I felt, as the minutes went by, an increasing tingling sensation all around, of which I told Luann.

"Put out your hands to your sides, with your palms up," she said. "And they will come to you."

I did as I was told.

I stood, transfixed, in the most aware state I can remember, and it seemed I did feel something come to me and a tingling in my hands and fingers.

A few minutes later, we went back to the house to look at the images that had been captured during our visit to the barn. To my astonishment, the photographs showed a definite progression of events. As mentioned, when we entered the barn at first, trampling hay everywhere, a couple of little dust orbs showed up in the digital camera frames of my fellow ghost hunters. It was when we were perfectly still, however, as Luann began her soothing monologue, that they began to gather. And the more she talked, the more she reassured her fairies, and the *more still we stood*, the more orbs gathered around me.

Sure enough, when she asked them to come to me, into my hands, there they were.

The barn was lit with the flashes of a dozen cameras, and their frames all captured the scene. When I looked at them, I was deeply quieted. In each one, there I was: standing, shivering in an Indiana barn at midnight, arms outstretched, with a rapturous expression on my face—and my hands filled with little balls of light.

Today, when we say a person "believes in fairies" it's become a blanketing way of saying that one is gullible, irrational, or easily duped. Yet, at the dawn of the 21st century, researchers are beginning to realize that many of the fanciful phenomena of years past may have a scientific reality that we are on the brink of discovering. But if even fairies turn out to be real, what will they be revealed as? The spirits of the dead? A tiny, flesh-and-blood species which has eluded us for millennia? Or something else? Less than a hundred years ago, one of the greatest minds of the time believed in the existence of ghosts, of psychic powers, and of fairies. Perhaps in one not-so-distant day, Arthur Conan Doyle—and his legions of modern-day followers—will be revealed as not so gullible after all.

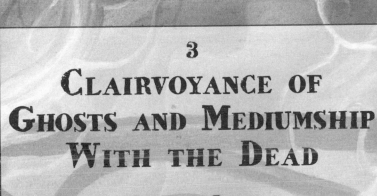

3

Clairvoyance of Ghosts and Mediumship With the Dead

Loved Ones

Ten years ago, after my older daughter, Eva, was born, I would occasionally observe a phenomenon that intrigues a lot of first-time parents. During particularly bad crying spells, when there seemed nothing that would comfort her, an extraordinary change would occur. Without reason, it seemed, she would suddenly become quiet, turn her head up toward the ceiling, and begin to smile or even break into laughter. These occurrences continued into Eva's first stage of talking, and in those days, the smiles would be accompanied by utterances of "gampa" or "gamma" or "unkow." We began to wonder if perhaps she was being consoled by her dad's deceased parents, or my late father, or one of her great uncles who had also passed.

Our wonderings took root as the incidences continued, and one afternoon, as I was out doing motherly errands, I got a surprise that seemed to validate our hunches. It was a warm, sunny fall afternoon, and Eva was just over a year old. We had gone shopping with my mom and, after dropping her off at home, made the leisurely, 20-minute drive back up toward our place to pick up the dry cleaning and stop for some groceries. Typically, by the time we arrived in our own neighborhood, Eva had fallen asleep in her car seat and, rather than wake her, I decided to just drive around for a bit and let her nap before making our stops.

Near our home was St. Adalbert Cemetery, where my father and his family are buried, and it's a sprawling, lovely place, so I made my way there to take a drive through the grounds. I turned in at the gate and followed the tree-lined road to the section where my dad had been interred nearly 20 years before. Near the site, I stopped the car and, before I could turn off the ignition, Eva joyfully called out from the backseat, "Grampa!"

I cannot count how many similar stories I have heard over the years from families convinced that their dead relatives and friends are lingering, but that the only evidence of it comes from the children who see them. Some psychics and clairvoyants believe that children, because of their very nature, are themselves a kind of lightning rod for ghosts in general, which would explain why, even in very intimate situations, children will see them while the adults in the situation will not. It's because spirits are actually attracted to children.

One Canadian medium, who maintains the blog *Dead Conversations* (*deadcon.blogspot.com*), has been seeing spirits for decades. Years of experience have taught him that

> bottom line, kids are more open. They are less jaded by the world, and more friendly...well, usually. They are also full of energy, and can unwittingly channel that energy into a beacon for spirits. Spirits tell me that those children are like big mushroom clouds of white hot energy with an exterior layer of light cyan, hard to ignore, easy to notice.

> ...So this big beacon of blue and white light draws a lot of spirits to them, so they have a higher probability of drawing a strong spirit to them.... Therefore they have a higher probability of seeing a spirit. Weak spirits cannot manifest in any way. The best they can do is whisper through static at the best mediums out there. Normal spirits can talk easily to mediums, and can manifest in small ways—colder air, hotter air, whispers, dreams, knocking over something light, making electronics flicker a bit, etc. Strong spirits can manifest—those spirits are the ones that you can hear, see, and sometimes even feel.... Of course there are varying degrees of strength and ability. Point

being: the more ghosts you attract, the more of a chance you have at seeing a Big Kahuna.

A Naval reservist I know, we'll call him John, related to me an astounding story several years ago. John had come home from the Gulf War in the 1990s and, several months after his return, his buddy Jeff followed. Circumstances in Jeff's life had changed since his deployment, and he had nowhere to stay in Chicago, so John generously offered Jeff the guest bedroom in his home. Jeff's stay was both wonderful and dreadful. As it turned out, Jeff was struggling with mental illness, and he moved between periods of high energy— during which he would help John's wife with the housework and delight John's two sons with his hilarious antics and horseplay—and deep depression, retreating to his room for sometimes days at a time.

Eventually, Jeff hanged himself in the house. The family, shocked, soon realized that their erstwhile boarder was still with them. In the weeks after the funeral, John's wife would regularly enter the basement laundry room to discover that the washing machine had been emptied of its wet load without her assistance, and that the clothes were dry and folded neatly, ready to be put away. The same was true of the dinner dishes that often mysteriously washed and put themselves away while John's wife was helping their sons with homework in the family room.

Such benevolence might have gone unaddressed forever, except that there were disturbing incidences, too. The most troubling was Jeff's tendency to hover around the two boys, who had enjoyed his company so much in life. Night after night, the boys would complain that Jeff was trying to get into bed with them, and that they even heard him sobbing next to them.

Most chilling for the parents was an incident that occurred at a family birthday party about six months after Jeff's suicide. After developing a roll of film taken at the party, John and his wife were looking through the shots when one of the photos made their blood run cold. The picture was a typical one, capturing the family around the kitchen table, with the grandmother preparing to blow out the candles on the birthday cake. In the photo were John and his wife, the grandmother and grandfather, and John's two boys. In the photo, John's oldest son is standing on one end of the group, and his hand is stuck out in the air to the side, reaching slightly up. When John asked the boy why he'd had his arm stuck out like that, his son answered, "I had my arm around Uncle Jeff."

GIFTED

Sometimes there is more at play than the natural tendency of ghosts to gravitate toward children. Sometimes a child is in the beginning stages of a spiritually gifted life, and it's up to his or her family to decide how to handle the revelation.

Many years ago, when I first began my career as a ghost hunter, I had the privilege of meeting a woman who was dealing with her very young son's fledgling clairvoyance—the gift of seeing (but not communicating with) spirits. Of course, the situation was entirely evocative of M. Night Shyamalan's immensely popular film *The Sixth Sense,* and little Michael was struggling to understand his gift just as

Haley Joel Osment's character had heroically done in the film.

The family first realized Michael's gift after a dear aunt passed away. At the time, Michael was about 10 years old. A week after the funeral, they paid a visit to the newly dug gravesite and, during their time in the cemetery, Michael claimed to view a group of women nearby who none of the adults could see. In the days that followed, there were numerous occasions when Michael reported seeing his dead aunt in the family's house. One evening, going into the kitchen for some milk before bed, he saw her under the kitchen table. Later that week, he entered his bedroom after school, and she was gleefully jumping on the bed. Early one Sunday morning, when his parents were walking the family's huge dog, Michael reported seeing his aunt crouching in the dog's cage in the garage.

Mary Ann Winkowski, an Ohio medium, was one of the inspirations for the enduringly popular television series *The Ghost Whisperer* and has gone on record speaking about her childhood experiences with mediumship. She claims that, as a little girl, her parents and other adults refused to believe her claims of spirit communication, but that at the age of 7, her empathic grandmother, a believer, began taking her to funerals to develop her gift. According to Winkowski, most individuals attend their own wakes and funerals, lingering until after their burial or cremation. Over the years, she has found that there is a space of approximately 72 hours in which a spirit can finish up its earthly business, observe and sometimes interact with its loved ones, and enter into "the light," believed to be Heaven. Winkowski claims that her training in this distinctive work began as a young girl, helping these "earthbound spirits" tidy their affairs and put their flawed relationships to rest, and encouraging them to "go to the light" before the door closed.

Opinions differ as to why some individuals continue to exhibit seemingly clairvoyant or mediumistic tendencies beyond the typical incidents of early childhood. Although many believers hold fast to the idea that these abilities are spiritual "gifts," the more scientific-minded search for a physiological mechanism. To this end, some theorists have suggested that the answer lies in the production of synapses in the brain. The human brain contains a vast number of chemical synapses, with young children having about 10/16 synapses (10,000 trillion), which declines as a child ages, stabilizing at 10/15 to 5 × 10/15 synapses (1,000 to 5,000 trillion). Perhaps paranormal abilities are not gifts, but the staying power of synapses in certain individuals.

Belief in this theory leads to other questions. For example, does one's environment determine whether synapses will decline or remain at a high level through adolescence and into adulthood? If a child is raised in a home open to the idea of the paranormal, will this supportive environment somehow encourage the continued high production of synapses? Conversely, if a child is raised in an environment hostile to paranormal belief, is the child's brain function actually affected? Is this, in fact, why so few in our society seem to have paranormal abilities?

The most popular theory by far among believers is, in fact, quite in line with this scientific theory, but without the scientific jargon. Most non-scientific researchers who have studied children's experiences with the paranormal believe that it is adult social norms that dictate what children do or do not paranormally perceive. Essentially, they follow our leads. They want to please us and not upset us. So children whose experiences with clairvoyance or mediumship are accepted by their parents, teachers, and other adults are more likely to continue to speak about these experiences and, essentially, incorporate them into their lives. Such children are also more likely, it seems, to continue to have such experiences into adulthood.

Worth mentioning is that some researchers connect injury with psi ability. This theory suggests that some individuals develop clairvoyance or mediumship after Near-death experiences (NDEs) or major physical trauma—usually head injury—which triggers psychic functioning in the brain. Believers suggest that the temporary "crossing over" to the afterlife leads to a permanent connection to that world after the experiencer is revived, allowing the individual to interact with interdimensional beings, including spirits of the dead, long after their recovery. Skeptics insist, however, that such alleged interactions are nothing but hallucinations, caused by head injuries or seizures of the temporal lobe of the brain.

INVISIBLE FRIENDS...AND ENEMIES

Many researchers—and parents themselves—have come to believe that at least some of the so-called "invisible friends" so prevalent in childhood history are actually the spirits of dead children.

Sometimes these spirits attach themselves to living children during cemetery visits, hospital visits or stays, or any forays into sites where children are dying or have recently died. If the dying or deceased individual is a child, the relationship may be a harmless or even beneficial one for the living child, providing friendship, companionship, and even instruction, as some spirit children have been known to teach their living playmates other languages or musical skills, and even help with homework. However, if the invisible friend is an adult spirit, the results can sometimes be quite harmful to the living child.

In her book *The Unquiet Dead*, Dr. Edith Fiore describes her experiences as a psychologist dealing with thousands of cases of so-called spirit possession. After working with many depressed, schizophrenic, and bipolar patients—most with self-destructive, negative tendencies—Fiore came to believe that an overwhelming number of such patients are actually possessed by spirits of the dead who attach themselves to a living body at the time of death, usually because of lingering anger and resentments in their lives, or because of fear of death itself.

Sometimes, the consequences of such attachment are incredibly dire. Trish Baldwin of Alberta, Canada, has first-hand experience with such an attachment:

Even as a small child I have always seen and heard things that nobody else could. My parents always chalked it up to "night scares" or an "over-active imagination." It wasn't until I moved out on my own at 17 and awoke to a man walking by my bedroom doorway, that my family starting admitting there was more than just an imagination at work. This realization came when the man I described was my dad's brother, who had passed before I was born. Being so sensitive, it wasn't a big surprise when later in life, my two daughters started coming to me with the same concerns that my parents would shrug off as "night scares."

When we moved into a newly built house, all was calm until the birth of my second daughter, Sierra. Something was in the hospital room and it wasn't nice—a horrible feeling with the appearance of what looked like a a human shape but when you looked through it—it looked as though you were looking through a bubble. I believe whatever it was followed me home and tormented my older daughter, Tristie, and I to the point I had to get the house blessed. This in itself is a whole different story.

After the Priest came with holy water and did the blessing, all was calm, but not for long. Tristie, at the age of 12, started complaining how a little girl kept shaking her bed, and peering over the end of the bed at her and giggling. Being a child, ghost or not, the antics started up. Rooms would be messed up, caps on bottles would spin off even when the lids were tight, and there was tugging at my clothes.

Even children in my day care would ask, "Where did the little girl go?" when there were no other children around because they were in school. I think the little ghost girl was shy because she would only show herself to one person at a time.

One quiet day, Sierra, who was 5, asked to play with my digital camera. It was just her and I home and it gave her something to do while I cooked supper. She played with it for a bit and then put the camera away. A couple days later, my sister was over and was looking through the pictures on the camera, when she looked at me and said, "There is a leg in the picture!" I looked and thought that was impossible! I literally ran and downloaded the pictures. What I saw shocked me. It looked as though Sierra caught something that didn't want to be seen. I saw a leg, part of a dress, and a slipper with a flower on it. I knew this wasn't either of my kids —my girls didn't like to wear dresses. And I didn't have any other kids in my home the day that the picture was taken. Many people that do not believe in ghosts have looked at the picture and are speechless. I always say if you have any logical explanation I will take it—no explanations have come yet. The picture was taken in 2003. I have since moved.

Recently, just a couple of weeks ago, my friend, who was also my neighbor, told me that the little antics are still going on to this day. She hasn't showed the new residents my picture. They are moving due to a job transfer, so we will see if the next people have the same experiences.

Trish Baldwin snapped this photo of her daughter's not-so-invisible friend in their home. Baldwin later came to believe that her daughter brought the spirit home after a hospital visit. (Photograph by Trish Baldwin.)

Deaths in the House

Child spirits from the outside world, then, do sometimes come home with children. Most often, however, spirits of children are attached to the places where they resided while alive. The classic cases involve children who underwent violent deaths at home. For American ghost researchers, one of the most intriguing haunted sites in the nation owes its reputation partly to the activity of a ghostly child who died in an appalling massacre by a still-unknown hand in the summer of 1912.

The Josiah Moore Home stands in the remote town of Villisca, Iowa, not far from the Nebraska border. Josiah and his wife, Sarah lived in the home with their children, Herman, age 11, Katherine, age 9, Boyd, age 7, and 5-year-old Paul. On the night of June 9th, the family attended a program at their local Presbyterian church, and then returned home, bringing along two neighboring children, Lena and Ina Stillinger, ages 12 and 8, to spend the night. At about 7:00 the next morning, the Moores' next door neighbor realized that the family's chores had not yet been started, and that the house seemed strangely still. A knock on the door received no answer, and she found, upon trying the knob, that the door had been locked from the inside. She called Josiah's brother, Ross Moore, who arrived on the scene with a key to gain them entry. He found Lena and Ina Stillinger in the bedroom off the parlor, their lifeless bodies across the bed and dark stains on the bedding. The sheriff was summoned. Upon arrival, the city marshall found the Moore family all dead in their beds. Like the Stillinger children, their skulls had been bludgeoned with an axe. Even now, the murders remain unsolved, though a number of suspects were fingered.

Villisca Axe Murder victims Josiah Moore and wife Sara with Herman and Katherine. The littlest victims, Boyd and Paul, had not yet been born. *(Photograph courtesy of Darwin and Martha Linn.)*

Today, the so-called Villisca Axe Murder House is a popular destination for crime buffs, morbid tourists, and paranormal researchers, especially the latter of whom have discovered what some believe to be paranormal residue of the brutal act. Photos of orbs—believed to be balls of spirit energy—have been taken in several areas of the house, and visiting psychics and clairvoyants claim that the spirit of the murderer inhabits the second-floor storage space, where the killer was believed to have hid while the family was at church. Most intriguing, however, is the spirit of the youngest victim, 5-year-old Paul Moore, who is believed to haunt the upstairs closet, in the room where his little body was found.

The author with ghost hunters Troy Taylor and David Rodriguez outside the Villisca Axe Murder House. (*Photograph by Anney Horn.*)

I was fortunate to be part of an investigation of the house one recent summer, which included among the investigators members of Paranormal Research and Investigative Studies Midwest (P.R.I.S.M.), a ghost-hunting group with several chapters around the heartland. The P.R.I.S.M. team had set up a video camera in the upstairs bedroom and a closed circuit monitor in the downstairs kitchen. Their focus was the door of the bedroom closet, which had been the center of curious activity in the past.

One of the investigators, Anney, had brought along a bag of candy to use as "bait" for the ghost of Paul Moore. Baiting is a paranormal investigation technique in which a desirable object, suited to the target spirit, is placed in the haunted area to encourage activity. Candy and toys are often used as bait for the ghosts of children. After placing the candy near the door, Anney asked Paul to open the door for her, telling him he could have the candy if he did so. After several minutes of coaxing, the door seemed to bounce or shake a little, like a runner flexing for a race, before it slowly swung open before our amazed eyes.

After we all examined the door and the closet, vainly looking for a draft or slope that could explain it, Anney closed the door again, placed the candy again, and resumed her conversation with Paul. Again, she asked him to open the door in exchange for the prize. Incredibly, after just a few moments, the door swung open a second time.

All present tried, again without success, to find an explanation for the movement. We all attempted to garner the same response, placing candy near the door and asking Paul to open it, yet none but Anney succeeded. Finally, we went downstairs to see if the door would open when no one was present, but over the course of two hours of monitoring via closed circuit television the door did not budge.

Paul Moore met a horrible death in his own home, but most child ghosts are simply attached to their homes after death, or even to life itself, even if they die of childhood illness or by accident. In fact, it's entirely possible that when children remain in their homes after death, it is because they are not aware they have died. This is also sometimes the case with adults who die, but children have a greatly reduced understanding of the "inappropriateness" of remaining in the physical world after death. They have not, for the most part, learned about death, about the possibilities of life after it, or about "moving on" or "into the light."

As a paranormal investigator, I have been contacted by a number of grieving families over the years who are alarmed to find that their dead children are still in the house. Their apparitions, voices, and movements of favorite objects all signal that these children have not moved on. Parents, anxious for their childrens' peace, want help in making that happen.

On every visit to each home, I have found the same situation. After introductions and formalities, I'm taken to the child's bedroom. Without fail, the rooms are unchanged. Books and toys remain where they were when the child was alive, the closets filled with clothes and shoes, and with stuffed animals and dolls on the bed. On more than one occasion, pajamas waited on the bedspread, as if the child would be tucked in at any moment, one last time.

It's no wonder these little spirits remain behind. In many cases, children's whole lives are focused on the home. They do not have jobs, and in some cases are not even in school yet. They have few contacts outside the home, and their dearest friends are their brothers and sisters, if they have them, also in the home. Even more compellingly, their first need is their parents, who remain in the home, very much alive, very appealing and comforting, especially in their unfamiliar new state of disembodiment. Unlike adults who die, children often have no familiar acquaintances who have passed away, so no parents, siblings, or friends are waiting to "cross them over."

Parents, too, often understandably keep their children's rooms just as they were in life, with all of their belongings in place, and in many cases they sleep in the child's bed or with the child's stuffed animals, or they spend time in the child's room, crying and talking to the dead child. All of these things serve to keep the child's spirit attached to the home.

Sometimes, the parents react quite conversely to a child's death, moving immediately out of the house and getting rid of all of the child's belongings. If a new family moves in and new children arrive, the dead child may become attracted and attached to the new child, toys, and books, and, ultimately, to the new family itself. The best course of action in the case of a child's death is to keep a memento of the child—a favorite stuffed toy is the obvious choice—and to move on with the family's life as well as possible.

THE SHADOW PEOPLE

One of the most talked about topics in current paranormal research circles is the subject of so called Shadow People or Shadow Men. The first time I heard of the phenomenon was in elementary school, when a friend of mine shared her experience of it. Each night, she said, for as long as she could remember, her mom would say goodnight, turn out the light, and close the bedroom door. A few minutes later, the closet door would swing slowly open, and a tall, shadowy male figure, dressed in a suit, would come out, walk over to the bed, smile at her, and return to the closet. The phenom-enon had gone on her whole life, each and every night, so by the time she told the story to me, she was completely used to the experience, though it made my blood run cold.

My friend's "Shadow Man in the Closet," as she called him, exhibited a number of the qualities commonly asso-ciated with Shadow People: his figure was darkish and not very well defined, he avoided adults and was attracted to children, and he seemed to "live" in the closet of the child's bedroom. Hearing my friend's story, one would assume she simply had a ghost in the house, perhaps a former tenant who hanged himself in the closet or some such thing, but most researchers have come to believe that these entities may be something entirely different.

Robert Bruce calls them "Negs"—shorthand for "nega-tive entities"—and believes they pose a very real danger to the living, especially the children to whom they seem so attracted. Bruce does not believe that Negs are ghosts, but that they are separate entities who were never alive in the physical world. According to Bruce, Negs do literally live in children's closets or under their beds, hiding from light and sound during the day and emerging at night to "feed" off the energy of spiritually defenseless children, leaving them physically lethargic, emotionally drained, and spiritually weak. It may sound ludicrous to suggest that there really are terrors under the bed and in the closet, the places children have traditionally feared at night, but research suggests that such fears may have a very real basis: that children are afraid of these places *not* because they don't know what's hiding there, but because they do.

For as long as I can remember, my daughters have made sure to close the bedroom closet door every night before turning in, no matter where we have lived. Indeed, researchers tell us that, in their experiences, closing the closet door securely actually goes a long way in quelling children's experiences with Shadow People. When Robert Bruce counsels parents on keeping Negs at bay, he advises the opposite, for a similar result: open the closet door or take it off its hinges, and put a night light inside. Likewise, he advises keeping beds free of bedskirts to keep the underside exposed, and keeping a lamp burning on the floor to help illuminate the space under the bed. Playing a radio softly, too, accomplishes two tasks: providing sound (anathema to Negs) and simulating the presence of adults, who Negs avoid because of their strong spiritual resistance.

Some researchers believe that Shadow People are much more than simply negative or parasitic entities, but that they are actively malevolent—demonic—in nature. Many encounters with Shadow People contain some distinctly dark commonalities. The appearance of the figure is very dark—sometimes described as "blacker than black"—and typically has no distinct shape; these figures are only recognizable as "people" because they have red eyes. One particularly malevolent manifestation, however, is very distinct: the so-called "Hat Man" who appears in a three-piece suit and fedora. Often accompanying the encounters are feelings of dread or simply "bad" feelings, feelings overwhelmingly described as evil or threatening by the experiencer. Worst of all, parents of children who encounter these entities say that their children undergo disturbing personality changes, becoming depressed or angry, and often losing interest in favorite subjects, hobbies, family activities, and friends. Some believe this is the beginning of demonic possession.

So what's to be done about these disturbing or even destructive entities? In addition to the previous suggestions of using light and noise at night to keep Negs at bay, Robert Bruce suggests that running water is a powerful force in separating Negs from children. The belief that ghosts and other unseen energies cannot cross water is an ancient one, but one that is often still invoked today (note that the sprinkling of holy water is a central part of the exorcism ritual). Then, according to Bruce, if a child is bothered in the night, a pass through the shower or even stepping over the garden hose while it's running can temporarily end the connection. If the Neg remains, engaging in one of these rituals regularly is believed to eventually force the Neg to seek another victim for its parasitic needs.

Heidi Hollis, a longtime researcher of Shadow People, believes that these entities have been living among us for many centuries and have been a constant dark influence upon the world. She offers many suggestions for driving them away from children, recommending that children be taught to let go of their fear and stand their ground against them, to focus on positive thoughts, to invoke the name of God or Christ when confronted by them, and—like Bruce—to keep lights on and regularly spray children's bedrooms with spring water.

However, if the Shadow Person is more than just negative (perhaps a demonic entity), more drastic measures may be needed to end the confrontations. Though some are tempted to seek the ritual of exorcism, the true, authentic exorcism ritual of the Roman Catholic or Episcopalian churches is very difficult to obtain permission for. However, many victims of Shadow People swear by the Roman Catholic "binding" prayer of St. Michael the Archangel. A binding prayer is believed to bind the forces of evil spirits, rendering them powerless:

> Saint Michael the Archangel, defend us in battle.
> Be our protection against the wickedness and snares of the devil.
> May God rebuke him, we humbly pray; and do Thou, O Prince of the Heavenly Host—by the Divine Power of God—cast into hell, satan and all the evil spirits, who roam throughout the world seeking the ruin of souls.

4
COMMUNICATION WITH
ANIMALS

Much of what we teach our children about paranormal ability comes from our portrayal of these abilities in folklore and literature. In recent years the stories of Harry Potter, the *Twilight* vampires and other paranormally affected characters have gone a long way in reducing the stigma, if not the sensationalism, of paranormal ability. But for centuries, and still today, one form of paranormal interaction still retains a questionable reputation: the ability to communicate with animals.

Modern fairytales and literature actually portray this ability as a sign of exceptional character. Snow White, Cinderella, Mary Poppins—each is able to discourse with birds, mice, and other creatures, and is a model moral character, full of virtue, existing on a higher spiritual plane than the other adults around them. But earlier stories present a different picture, suggesting that the ability to communicate with animals is an evil one.

The story of the Pied Piper of Hamelin is one still told today, though infrequently. It is the story of a traveling musician, a piper dressed in a colorful (pied) costume, who enters a town that has become overrun by rats. The piper approaches the town council and offers to rid the town of the rodents, in exchange for a fee. The council agrees to the terms, and the piper successfully leads the rats out of town, by playing a hypnotic piping tune that makes them follow. Returning to the town to collect his fee, the council refuses to pay. As payback, the piper begins his tune again, but this time all the children of the town follow him out and away, never to be seen again.

What appears to be a simple story, teaching a moral lesson, actually has its basis in a real, though mysterious event that occurred in the city of Hamelin, Germany, on June 26, 1284. The earliest mention of the story seems to have been through a depiction of it on a stained glass window in the Hamelin Church, which was placed in the year 1300 and was later destroyed. According to descriptions of the window in historical documents, it portrayed the colorfully dressed Piper and several children dressed in white. Encircling the glass was the testimony:

> IN THE YEAR 1284, ON THE DAYS OF JOHN AND PAUL, IT WAS THE 26TH OF JUNE, CAME A COLORFUL PIPER TO HAMELN AND LED CXXX CHILDREN AWAY

Incredibly, Hamelin's town records are dated from the date of the tragedy. From 1351, entries in the Hamelin book of statutes are dated according to the number of years "after our children left." But while the window was believed to have been created to memorialize a tragic event in the city's history, no clear record of the event exists, though theories abound.

The oldest picture of the Pied Piper copied from the glass window of the Market Church in Hamelin Germany. Painting by Augustin von Moersperg (1592). *(Wikimedia Commons.)*

Some historians believe the children were either drowned in the Weser River or buried alive in a landslide. Others wonder if the children contracted a disease, possibly an early form of Black Death, and were led out of town to avoid spreading the disease to the adult inhabitants. Possibly, the children were victims of an outbreak of chorea, or communal dancing mania, a number of which were recorded during the time of the Plague. It may be that the Piper was not a physical figure at all, but a representation of the Devil, who "led the children away" through disease.

Though these stories are intriguing, most scholars have come to believe that the children of Hamelin were part of the colonization of Europe and founded their own towns in the eastern regions. Some eastern towns bear names like Querhamelm ("mill village Hamelin") and other references to "Hamelin." These theories suggest that the Piper was a recruiter or organizer of the colonists—in this case, the Hamelin children.

Though the earliest accounts of the Piper story do not include any reference to rats, later, written accounts included them, presumably to make the Piper appear more sinister, because he was able to communicate with animals—and not just any animals, but those who had brought the Black Death upon the continent.

The idea of talking animals as evil stems from the book of Genesis itself, and the tale of the serpent persuading Eve to eat the fruit of the Tree of Life. Interestingly, Eve had the ability to speak with animals before the Fall, when she existed on a higher spiritual plane, but she lost the ability after disobeying God and eating the fruit. So, confusingly, her heightened spiritual level made her able to speak with animals, but that very ability was her ruin. It's understandable, indeed, that the ability to speak with animals gained a sorry reputation.

Cats, in particular, have sometimes endured— and still maintain to some extent a cultural connection to evil, stemming surely from the Medieval associa-

The Serpent Tempting Eve. Henry Fuseli, 1802. *(Wikipedia.)*

tion of cats with witches. Cats belonging to known or supposed witches were called familiars, from the word *famulus,* which means a servant or slave. The Church itself decreed that familiars were demons in animal form, and it was believed that these demon-animals were given as gifts by the Devil at a witch's initiation. It was widely believed that familiar animals could speak with humans, and that they were often sent to deliver messages where the witch herself could not tread. Black cats, in particular, were the main targets of anti-cat campaigns, as many believed that *all* black cats were the Devil's, not just the familiars. Reportedly, Pope Innocent VII passed a law that all cats in Europe were to be put to death, which led to the deaths of many cats—and their owners, all believed to be witches.

In 1931, a bizarre creature was said to have overturned the normalcy of the Irving family, who lived on a farm near the hamlet of Dalby on Britain's Isle of Man. Gef the Talking Mongoose—otherwise known as the Dalby Spook—could only be seen by the family's 13-year-old daughter, Voirrey, though the rest of the family experienced Gef's hijinks. At first, the family reported scratching noises in the walls. Though they first thought they had a rat in the house, Gef then began making other sounds, such as growling or gurgling. It wasn't long before Gef began to speak English. The invisible thing said it was a mongoose from New Delhi, that its name was Gef, and that he had come to England in 1852. Voirrey described the creature as very much unlike a mongoose: a yellowish thing, sized like a rat, and with a bushy tail. Gef told the family he was an earthbound spirit and "a ghost in the form of a weasel." On one bizarre occasion he cried, "I am a freak! I have hands and I have feet, and if you saw me you'd faint! You'd be terrified, mummified, turned into stone or a pillar of salt!"

Paranormal researchers were fascinated when the story spread through England, as Gef performed many physical actions reminiscent of poltergeist activity, such as throwing objects. James Irving, Voirrey's father, kept a journal about Gef's activities for three years, which he gave to the famous English ghost investigator Harry Price, who investigated the case with journalist Rex Lambert. Price took impressions of Gef's alleged footprints and teeth marks, which were analyzed by London's Natural History Museum and reportedly found to be unidentifiable.

Nandor Fodor was another famed investigator of the paranormal who examined the case of Gef. Fodor was the first to theorize that poltergeists are actual displaced energy from a living agent rather than spirits of the dead. In this case, it would have been likely that Voirrey—an adolescent—was the poltergeist agent. Fodor lived with the Irvings for a week without experiencing anything unusual; however, testimony of neighbors and other witnesses convinced him of the case's authenticity.

James Irving with daughter Voirrey outside Doarlish Cashen, their home on the Isle of Man, which they were said to have shared with Gef the Talking Mongoose.

Among the more interesting statements Mr. Irving recorded in his journal was: "I am not evil. I could be if I wanted. You don't know what damage or harm I could do if I were roused. I could kill you all, but I won't." When a family member asked where Gef would go when he died, he replied: "To Hell, to the Land of Mist."

The Irving family sold their farm in 1937. Almost 10 years later, the new owner claimed to have shot Gef; however the corpse was black and white and larger than the "mongoose" described by Voirrey years before. She died in 2005, still claiming that Gef was real.

In 1974 Gerard and Laura Goodin contacted famed paranormal investigator Lorraine Warren and her late husband, Ed, about recent activity in the Goodins' Bridgeport, Connecticut home. For weeks, the family had been plagued by all sorts of unusual activity, they claimed, including the movement and levitation of objects, desecration of religious artifacts, and the transformation of the family cat. According to their story, their 10-year-old daughters' pet cat, Sam, had recently undergone surgery and then had begun acting peculiarly and, one day, talking in a human voice and shouting racial slurs.

The daughter, Marcia, was an adopted child, overprotected by her adoptive parents and described both as deceitful and desirous of attention. The case of the so-called Lindley Street haunting gained national attention after police visits to the house appeared in the local police blotter. After an ongoing investigation by the Warrens and visits from a number of religious practitioners and students of demonology, it was decided the case was likely a combination of poltergeist activity centered around the troubled little girl, evil spirits drawn to her angry, negative energy, and fraudulent activity deliberately caused by the girl herself. Late in the case, the girl confessed to moving objects when no one was looking and to making the cat "talk" through ventriloquism, but most eyewitnesses claimed that only some of the phenomena could have been fraudulent. The early events, they maintained, were genuine, and the later, fraudulent ones were created by the daughter so that the attention would continue. Neither the Warrens nor other investigators ever expressed whether they believed the talking cat to be a demonic manifestation or a poltergeist-related event.

Today, the fear of speaking with animals is being replaced by a quite different attitude. In the *Harry Potter* series of books, Harry is a parselmouth—that is, a person who can speak with snakes in snake language (Parseltongue), so of course children today think this is a great ability. But adults, too, are starting to look at child-animal communication as a positive ability, largely because of studies of autistic children.

Many paranormal researchers and specialists in autism have come to believe that both animals and autistic children exist on a higher spiritual or intuitive plane, allowing them to sometimes communicate without the use of speech or other "normal" means. But whereas autistic children seem to maintain this ability into adulthood, most children seem to have some of this ability, at least for awhile. We will look at the special and extraordinary relationship between autistic children and animals separately, but for a moment let's examine an instance of child-animal communication in "normal" children.

One summer when I was 4 years old, we had a whole litter of rabbits fenced in a huge hutch in the backyard of our house. "My" rabbit was a baby white rabbit for whom I held a special affection. One morning, after my dad and I had come in from feeding the rabbits and I was coloring in the dining room, I began to feel nervous and agitated for no apparent reason. After a few minutes, I was overcome with a feeling of panic about my rabbit, and sure enough, when I ran outside to check on it, I found that, when we had lowered the fence after the feeding, my rabbit had gotten its neck caught underneath and could not get out. Well, my rabbit died, but I couldn't help but think that I had known it was in distress because of our special attachment.

I discovered over the years that many children have these special empathic connections with their pets, and that they actually feel the pain of their pets and see mental pictures of them when they are in trouble. A number of children also experience clairaudience (paranormal hearing) of animals this way. They will actually hear their pets ask for things they need or want, and I've even encountered families in which children who are waiting for daddy to come home that "heard" their dad was stuck in traffic or had gotten into an accident, only to have this revealed as true.

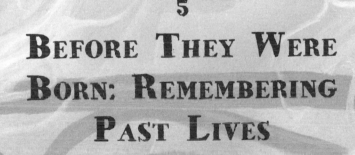

5

BEFORE THEY WERE BORN: REMEMBERING PAST LIVES

To die will be an awfully big adventure.

—Peter Pan

Reincarnation research is an area of parapsychological study that investigates claims of "transmigration of the soul", that is, the transfer of the personality from one body to another at the time of, or sometime after, bodily death. Like much of parapsychology, skeptics hold that no evidence has demonstrated the reality of reincarnation, and so the study of it is still considered pseudoscientific, not real science.

HYPNOTIC REGRESSION

Hypnotic regression has been one major line of inquiry into the curious claims of the "reincarnated." Under hypnosis, the "memories" that subjects share are absolutely the same as their verifiable memories, detailed and convincing. However, critics accuse them of being generated by cryptonesia or "unconscious plagiarism" of other people's life events. Some believe that the past life memories are merely confabulations: the unconscious melding of experiences, learned information, and suggestion to form believable stories.

The first person to popularize the use of hypnotic regression to discover past lives was an amateur hypnotist from Colorado named Morey Bernstein. In 1952, Bernstein hypnotized a local woman, Virginia Tighe, with the goal of using hypnotic regression to take her back *past* her birth to see what would happen. Incredibly, Bernstein led Tighe back through her earliest years, backward through her very birth, to a previous life.

Under hypnosis, Tighe introduced herself as "Bridey Murphy," an 8-year-old girl living in County Cork, in early-19th-century Ireland. She recounted the events of her life, including her marriage to an attorney, her later life in the city of Belfast, and, eventually, her death from a fatal fall. While hypnotized, Tighe described her grave and tombstone, and the numbness of the disembodied state that followed bodily death. Though she remembered her rebirth as Tighe, many years later, in the United States, she could not recall the mechanism or circumstances by which it had occurred.

Bernstein published his work with Tighe in a hugely popular book entitled *The Search for Bridey Murphy*, a classic of parapsychology. But the "memories" that Bridey shared in the regression sessions did not pan out. The sensational claims of Bernstein sent many of the curious in search of Bridey, but what most found was much less compelling than the book that started it all. Scores of newspapers and periodicals dispatched reporters to Ireland to fact check the details of Bridey's story. No record of her birth or death could be found, her house could not be located, and the church she said she'd attended had not been built until almost 50 years after Bridey's claimed demise. However, a few details were shockingly accurate, including a description of the Antrim coast, particulars of the route between Belfast and Cork, and the name of the local grocer of the time.

Because of the conflicting evidence, the battle between believers and disbelievers continued—for a while. However, the case seemed closed when a journalist discovered that, as a child growing up in Chicago, Tighe had lived across the street from an Irish immigrant named Bridie Murphy Corkell, convincing researchers that all of "Bridey's" memories were those of Tighe's own childhood.

CHILDREN'S PAST LIVES

Of most interest to serious researchers have been cases of apparent reincarnation that are revealed *without* hypnosis, particularly by children. Often, children who talk about previous lives grow up to actually verify the details of the lives they've remembered since infancy, and even to find physical correlations between their bodies and the bodies of the deceased.

Without question, the most compelling evidence for reincarnation comes from the life's work of the late Dr. Ian Stevenson, a Montreal-born biochemist and psychiatrist who, early on, took issue with the limitations of traditional medical practice. In the late 1950s, Stevenson was first exposed to what are called "cases suggestive of reincarnation." He was most impressed by one factor: that the first suggestion of reincarnation often occurs under the age of 10. Stevenson began actively interviewing children with such experiences. After his first paper on the subject was published, he was invited by well-known psychic Eileen J. Garrett to undertake an in-depth study of children in India and Sri Lanka. Central to Stevenson's work was the financial support of Chester Carlson, who later created a chair at the University of Virginia, Charlottesville, and left $1 million to support Stevenson's future work. With the funds, Stevenson founded the Division of Personality Studies (later, the Division of Perceptual Studies)—a departmental division dedicated to research into the still-unknown relationships between matter and mind: parapsychology. Stevenson, however, was boldly opposed to the term *parapsychology* in relation to the division's work. He believed that the efforts of he and his colleagues were, rather, an outgrowth of traditional science and medicine, and not properly termed as parapychological research.

Stevenson spent decades collecting cases of possible reincarnation, mostly those claimed by children, traveling tens of thousands of miles each year, to Europe, Africa, India, and the Americas. Throughout, he found that children typically began to talk of past lives at a very young age—sometimes as early as 2—with very specific detail about the way their former bodies had died. Often, the previous life seemed to be that of a family member who had passed away before the child was born. Almost always, a violent death was to blame.

Throughout his life, and after his death, proponents of Stevenson's research hold fast to his scientific propriety. Just as Stevenson himself separated his work from parapsychology, his allies maintain that his work was staunchly and traditionally scientific, and squarely launched from skepticism to the very end. This quality was lauded by journalist Tom Shroder, who followed Stevenson on his case-finding expeditions for months and documented the trip in his book, *Old Souls*. Shroder likened Stevenson's methodology to that of a reporter or detective, harshly dismissing anything remotely unverifiable as useless. Still, case after case baffled him—and his companion.

When the expedition began, Shroder was a skeptic "in the gut," an unbeliever because he could not "feel the possibility" of reincarnation:

> In my marrow, I could feel no trace, however faint, of a previous life. The universe before me was a void, a nothingness that flared into somethingness only with my earliest memories of this life. And my most profound learning about the deaths of the people I had loved the most was this: They had vanished.

Despite reservations, as the journey progressed, Shroder became increasingly confounded by case after case. Most remarkable was the story of a Beirut woman named Suzanne Ghanem, who claimed to be the reincarnation of Hanan Mansour, a woman from a neighboring town who had died during heart surgery 10 days before Suzanne was born.

At the age of 16 months, Suzanne picked up the phone receiver and said, "Hello, Leila?" Years later, when they found the family of Hanan Mansour—a real woman who had died just the way Suzanne said—they also found her daughter, Leila, who Hanan had tried to call before her fatal surgery. As a toddler, Suzanne continued to insist she was not Suzanne, but Hanan, and when her parents asked, "Hanan who?" she said her head wasn't big enough to remember yet. But by the time she was 2, Suzanne had spoken of her "children" by name, and had longed for her "husband," Farouk, many times.

Eventually, the two families met, and the meetings became common. The Mansour family soon became convinced that Suzanne's story was true, and they felt responsible for her, especially in light of what appeared to be a deep sadness in the girl. When they were together, even at the age of 5, Suzanne would sit in Farouk Mansour's lap, leaning her head against his chest. When Farouk became engaged to one of Hanan's former friends, Suzanne was heartbroken. "You told me you'd never love anyone but me," she cried. Twenty years later, when Shroder and Stevenson revisited her, Suzanne was still alone and still very much in love with Farouk, who she yet called "my husband."

Robert Alameder, an American philosopher of science, became a staunch advocate of Stevenson's work, and urged scientists to recognize the profound value of his research. Alameder believed, like Stevenson, that the work had been misunderstood as on-the-fringe pseudoscience, and that a look at the actual research and methodology would convince many of the validity of Stevenson's results. Essentially, Alameder—like Stevenson—seemed to be passionately rallying for science to look *scientifically* at something that had never been seen as scientific: the human soul, and the possibility of its physical re-embodiment after bodily death:

> There is something essential to some human personalities, however we ultimately characterize it, which we cannot plausibly construe solely in terms of either brain states, or properties of brain states, or biological properties caused by the brain and, further, after biological death this non-reducible essential trait sometimes persists for some time, in some way, in some place, and for some reason or other, existing independently of the person's former brain and body. Moreover, after some time, some of these irreducible essential traits of human personality, for some reason or other, and by some mechanism or other, come to reside in other human bodies either some time during the gestation period, at birth, or shortly after birth.

Central to Stevenson's work was the attempt to correlate the experiences and memories of subjects with apparent physical traces of their former lives. Often, photographs of the previous personality bore striking resemblance—sometimes nearly

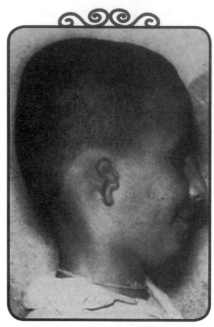

Severely malformed ear (microtia) of a Turkish boy who said that he remembered the life of a man who was fatally wounded on the right side of the head by a shotgun discharged at close range. (Reprinted from Ian Stevenson, "Birthmarks and Defects Corresponding to Wounds on Deceased Persons." Published in the *Journal of Scientific Exploration*, Vol. 7, No.4, pp. 403-410, 1993. Published by the Society for Scientific Exploration. *www.scientificexploration.org*.)

identical—to the grown child who claimed reincarnation. Even more interesting were the cases in which birthmarks and defects seemed present in the child at the site of the previous personality's death wounds. In 1992, Stevenson presented a paper entitled "Birthmarks and Defects Corresponding to Wounds on Deceased Persons" to the annual meeting of the Society for Scientific Exploration. The paper was published in the *Journal of Scientific Exploration* and presented a number of Stevenson's remarkable cases which seemed to combine experiential evidence with physical proof:

A Thai woman had three separate linear hypopigmented scar-like birthmarks near the midline of her back;

as a child she had remembered the life of a woman who was killed when struck three times in the back with an ax. (Informants verified this mode of death, but no medical record was obtainable.) A woman of Burma was born with two perfectly round birthmarks in her left chest; they slightly overlapped, and one was about half the size of the other. As a child she said that she remembered the life of a woman who was accidentally shot and killed with a shotgun. A responsible informant said the shotgun cartridge had contained shot of two different sizes. (No medical record was obtainable in this case.)

Another Burmese child said that she remembered the life of her deceased aunt, who had died during surgery for congenital heart disease. This child had a long, vertical linear hypopigmented birthmark close to the midline of her lower chest and upper abdomen; this birthmark corresponded to the surgical incision for the repair of the aunt's heart. (I obtained a medical record in this case.) In contrast, a child of Turkey had a horizontal linear birthmark across the right upper quadrant of his abdomen. It resembled the scar of a surgeon's transverse abdominal incision. The child said that he remembered the life of his paternal grandfather, who had become jaundiced and was operated on before he died. He may have had a cancer of the head of the pancreas, but I could not learn a precise medical diagnosis.

Two Burmese subjects remembered as children the lives of persons who had died after being bitten by venomous snakes, and the birthmarks of each corresponded to therapeutic incisions made at the sites of the snakebites on the persons whose lives they remembered. Another Burmese subject also said as a child that she remembered the life of a child who had been bitten on the foot by a snake and died. In this case, however, the child's uncle had applied a burning cheroot to the site of the bite—a folk remedy for snakebite in parts of Burma; and the subject's birthmark was round and located at the site on the foot where the bitten child's uncle had applied the cheroot.

In addition to the curious physical connections, Stevenson also often found apparent links between the children's behaviors and those of the people whose lives they remembered. For example, a child might carry on a previous grudge against a family member or dote on a husband as his dead wife once had, though there was no connection in the present lifetime. Many of the children also suffered from debilitating phobias reflective of the manner of death in the previous life, the majority associated with violent ends and the knives, guns, cars, or machinery that caused their deaths. Interestingly, a number of children were observed at play, pretending to be involved in the occupation of the previous life, though at the time they had no knowledge of the person's work. Still others would eerily and often reenact their deaths.

In the end, Stevenson stated that the thousands of cases he had collected—around 3,000—certainly did more than hint at the plausibility of reincarnation. Still, he would always term them "suggestive of reincarnation" because of the

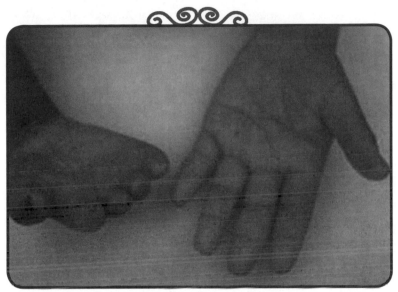

Almost absent fingers (brachydactyly) on one hand of a boy of India who said he remembered the life of a boy of another village who had put his hand into the blades of a fodderchopping machine and had its fingers amputated. (Reprinted from Ian Stevenson, "Birthmarks and Defects Corresponding to Wounds on Deceased Persons." Published in the *Journal of Scientific Exploration*, Vol. 7, No.4, pp. 403–410, 1993. Published by the Society for Scientific Exploration. *www.scientificexploration.org*.)

absence of knowledge of a physical process or mechanism by which it occurred: the fatal scientific flaw.

Carol Bowman is an American counselor specializing in children's past life memories. Her first book, *Children's Past Lives,* took Ian Stevenson's work into the popular realm and quickly became a New Age sensation. In the book, Bowman anecdotally shares numerous cases of children who have seemingly reincarnated, but with a markedly unscientific eye. The stories are sometimes puzzling, sometimes wondrous, often chilling. Bowman admits that most children talk about being other people in other places, but this is simply a part of the growing intellect of childhood. She offers four criteria for establishing a child's behavior as genuinely evidential of a past life. First, the behavior and information are presented matter-of-factly. There is no sensationalism about it. For example, one little girl was believed to have been her alcoholic grandmother reincarnated. On one occasion, the girl told her mother (previously, it seems, her daughter) that "I did not like you when you were my little girl." When the mother asked her why, she responded, "You always used to yell at me, and push me into my room and lock the door." As it turns out, the mother used to lock her mom in her room when she would drink too much, letting her out only when she'd slept it off. The girl's mother pointed out to Carol Bowman that, whenever her daughter was about to make a statement about her past life, she leaned close and whispered it seriously, sometimes taking her mother's face in her hands and looking into her eyes.

Another commonality to past life memories or behavior, according to Bowman, is consistency over time. Far from the spontaneous and short-lived scenes that children act out in games of pretend—or the more long-term identification of some children with superheroes, movie characters, or other imaginary personas—identification with a past life begins during a child's earliest speaking and behavior and lasts usually until the ages of 5 to 7.

According to Bowman, an obvious necessity in "proving" a child's past life is knowledge beyond experience.

Bowman's most publicized case remains that of little James Leininger, who as a small boy growing up in Louisiana, began to have recurrent nightmares about "his" plane crashing. "Airplane crash! Plane on fire! Little man can't get out!" he would cry from his crib each night, until one day—at still only 2 years of age—he told his baffled parents that the Japanese had shot down his plane.

Over time James would "reveal" that he had formerly existed as James Huston, Jr., a pilot who had been shot down during the battle of Iwo Jima. When questioned about the ship he worked with, he flatly said, "Natoma," possibly referring to the U.S.S. *Natoma Bay*, where a real pilot, Ensign James Huston, Jr., had been stationed during World War II until his fiery and fatal crash during the conflict at Iwo Jima. Later, James would meet some of the survivors of the battle—men who had known James Huston, Jr.—embracing them on sight as if seeing old friends.

When James was 3, he had started drawing pictures of battle scenes, with fighter planes and bombs exploding. The planes and weaponry were eerily detailed, and James pointed out the differences by name: showing his parents the Wildcats and Corsairs he had drawn, naming them as well as the Japanese enemy planes he'd included. James explained that the fighter planes were given boys' names and the bombers female names, a detail that, incredibly, was true. When he signed these drawings, James always wrote, in shaky crayon, "James 3." When his parents asked why, he said, "Because I am the third James."

The final criterion mentioned by Bowman for validating an authentic past life is the presence of corresponding behavior or traits. James Leininger had a habit, for example, of buckling his seat belt and then making a motion around his head that simulated the fastening of headgear, as if he were preparing for flight. He also frequently saluted for no reason. Other children—especially those believed to have reincarnated from family members—notably exhibit behaviors and personalities of their former personalities, including attitudes toward family members. Recall little Suzanne from Beirut who would nuzzle her head against her former "husband's" chest and express jealousy when speaking about his new wife. Bowman writes about a young boy—believed to have reincarnated from his grandmother—who shared his grandmother's penchant for elephants, though he had never met her or known anything about her.

Of course, skeptical rebuttals abound to confront the claims of young people like James and Suzanne, who seem uncannily tied to those who have since passed on. The less skeptical wonder if there is some sort of clairvoyance or telepathy involved, in which these children are picking up on the thoughts and events of the people they claim to have been. Are the memories of the dead or their grieving loved ones somehow "getting into the heads" of children, especially those born into the family of the deceased? Another possibility, if one is willing to believe, is that the actual spirit of the dead loved one is somehow possessing the child, filling her head with images and "memories" that are revealed in eerie ways.

Obviously, these theories demand a great deal of credulity of paranormal possibilities. True skeptics believe that past life "memories" and "behaviors" are acquired like any other knowledge or influence: through direct experience. Critics of the claims of little James Leininger are convinced that a visit to an aviation museum at the age of 18 months was all it took to set the wheels in motion. The typical boyhood fascination with planes and battles, the "leading" questions of credulous parents and therapists, and the father's growing collection of books and other materials detailing names, dates, and aircraft of the time: surely, the skeptics say, all of these joined to create a monstrous fantasy world. In the case of Suzanne Ghanem, certainly the girl learned of Hanan Monsour's family through overheard conversations, perhaps even between strangers at the market or out at play, filled with detail about a woman who had died in surgery.

But what of the mysterious birthmarks uncovered by the research of Ian Stevenson, mirroring the fatal wounds of the alleged past life personalities? Coincidence, the skeptics scoff, time and time again.

Still, despite continuing disbelief from traditional science—and the absence of a known mechanism for the reincarnation, many colleagues of Stevenson—as well as those with their own experiences of past life phenomena—believe that his research will one day be recognized as utterly groundbreaking: the first real evidence at the reality behind the so-called "pseudoscience" of reincarnation studies.

6

SEEING AND BELIEVING: CHILD VISIONARIES AND RELIGIOUS APPARITIONS

During the past century and a half, the Christian authorities—the Roman Catholic Church in particular—have examined scores of so-called apparitions, or sightings of and conversations with prominent spiritual beings. Overwhelmingly, the apparitions appear to be that of a beautiful "lady," presumably the Blessed Virgin Mary of Catholic doctrine. Less common are apparitions of St. Michael the Archangel, other angels and saints and, rarely, the figure of Christ or the Christ Child Himself. Overwhelmingly, religious apparitions are experienced by young people, usually those going through puberty, but occasionally teenagers.

When I was a little girl, my Aunt Frances was deeply devoted to the Blessed Virgin Mary, spending time each morning and evening saying special prayers in her honor and pursuing as much knowledge as possible about this fascinating woman, believed by most Christians to be the mother of God. Aunt Frannie used to take my mother, my brother, and me with her on road trips to Marian shrines near and far, and I think that these trips are partly responsible for instilling in me such a lifelong fascination with—and adherence to—the Church.

Today, I still vividly remember learning of the apparitions reported at Garabandal, Spain, in the 1960s, by four impoverished schoolgirls who shook up the tiny village for four years. Beginning with the first apparition in 1961, the girls reportedly experienced thousands of apparitions, first of the Archangel St. Michael, and then of the Blessed Virgin Mary. Untold numbers converged on the apparitional site, a grove of pine trees outside the village, and followed the girls through the winding, rocky streets, where they often walked or ran while in ecstasy (a rapturous spiritual state), sometimes backward, their heads thrown dangerously back, not watching where they were going, but never once stumbling or falling. As a young girl, I attended informational lectures about Garabandal, and I watched the film of the girls' ecstasies, heard the frightening prophesies given the girls regarding

The Garabandal seers in ecstasy. *(Photograph courtesy of GarabandalArchives.com.)*

the end of the world, and saw amazing photographs of alleged paranormal phenomena, including a remarkable capture of a Communion host that reportedly appeared on the tongue of one of the seers during an apparition.

When I was a teenager, we visited Necedah, Wisconsin, site of a deeply controversial series of alleged apparitions to a woman named Mary Ann Van Hoof, which began in 1949. The Roman Catholic Church launched an investigation into the events and declared them fraudulent. The Church instructed Van Hoof to cease her claims, and for her advocates to abandon support of them; however, they refused. As a result, Van Hoof was put under interdict—that is, she was forbidden from worshipping in public or receiving the sacraments of the Church, such as Holy Communion or Reconciliation.

In Marian apparitions, there is usually no physical contact between the seer and the apparitional being, but sometimes a PPA (permanent paranormal object) is left behind; for example, the case of the famed apparitions at Fatima, Portugal, when the popular image of Our Lady of Guadalupe was said to have been supernaturally imprinted on the robe of visionary Juan Diego.

According to the Catholic Church, "approved" apparitions (that is, apparitions deemed genuine by the Church) are matters of private spirituality. That is, there is no obligation on the part of the Church's members to accept the legitimacy of the apparitions. As a condition, apparitional messages may not affect or change Church doctrine or practice. According to reports, of almost 300 reported apparitions examined by the Church, only a dozen have been approved as genuine by the Vatican.

One of the Garabandal visionaries receives "mystical Communion" on her tongue during an ecstasy. *(Photograph courtesy of GarabandalArchives.com.)*

OUR LADY OF LASALETTE

The apparitions of Our Lady of LaSalette (France) were experienced by two shepherd children, Mélanie Calvat and Maximin Giraud, in 1846. Following the apparitions, a flood of reports circulated of healings surrounding the children and the site of the apparitions. The Roman Catholic Church investigated the claims and found them to be basically credible, though controversy arose years later concerning the legitimacy of the so-called "Secrets of LaSalette."

Years after the apparitions, Calvat carefully documented the events of the day leading up the apparitions, and painstakingly detailed the messages and secrets given to the children on the day in question. Her account is a moving one, partially detailed here:

On the 18th of September (1846), the eve of the Holy Apparition of the Holy Virgin, I was alone, as usual, watching over my Master's cows. Around eleven o'clock in the morning, I saw a small boy walking towards me. I was frightened at this, for it seemed to me that everyone ought to know that I avoided all kinds of company. This boy came up to me and said: 'Little girl, I'm coming with you.' At these words, the natural evil in me soon showed itself, and taking a few steps back, I told him: 'I don't want anybody around. I want to be alone.' But the boy followed me, saying: 'Go on, let me stay with you. My Master told me to come and watch over my cows together with yours.' I walked away from him, gesturing to him that I didn't want anybody around, and when I was some distance away, I sat down on the grass. There, I used to talk with the little flowers of the Good Lord. A moment later, I looked behind me, and there I found Maximin sitting close to me. Straightway he says to me: 'Keep me with you. I'll be very good.' But the natural evil in me will not hear reason. I jump to my feet, and run a little farther off without saying a word and again I start playing with the little flowers of the Good Lord. In an instant, Maximin was there again, telling me he would be very good, that he wouldn't talk, that he would get bored all by himself, and that his Master had sent him to be with me, etc. This time, I took pity, I gestured to him to sit down, and I kept on playing with the little flowers of the Good Lord.

She befriends the little boy, and the two meet the next morning to watch over their cattle together. After a long day, they fall asleep in the grass. She recalls:

When I woke up I couldn't see the cows, so I called Maximin and climbed up the little mound. From there I could see our cows grazing peacefully and I was on my way down, with Maximin on his way up, when all at once I saw a beautiful light shining more brightly than the sun. 'Maximin, do you see what is over there? Oh! My God!'

At the same moment, I dropped the stick I was holding. Something inconceivably fantastic passed through me in that moment and I felt myself being drawn. I felt a great respect, full of love, and my heart beat faster. I kept my eyes firmly fixed on this light, which was static, and as if it had opened up, I caught sight of another, much more brilliant light which was moving, and in this light I saw a most beautiful lady....

This beautiful Lady stood up; she coolly crossed her arms while watching us, and said to us: 'Come, my children, fear not, I am here to proclaim great news to you.' These soft and sweet words made me fly to her, and my heart desired to attach itself to her forever.

As the "lady" begins to speak, she reveals a number of unsettling prophecies:

Statue of Our Lady of La Salette talking to Mélanie Calvat and Maximin Giraud at Puy-de-Dôme, France. *(Photograph by Romary, Wikimedia Commons.)*

A great famine will come. Before the famine comes, children under the age of seven will begin to tremble and will die in the arms of those who hold them. The others will do penance through hunger. The nuts will go bad, the grapes will become rotten.

After these prophecies, the lady becomes silent to Melanie, but continued to speak to Maximim. Later, Melanie would learn that this was the moment when the boy was receiving his "secret": one of two messages of warning given the children during the course of the apparitions. Immediately after, turning back to the girl, the lady gives Melanie her own secret, along with instructions to make it public in the year 1858.

The secret, quite extensive, chastises at many levels. It begins with an admonition against priests and their "wicked lives" and goes on to scold world leaders, threatening "divisions among those who reign in every society." The secret directly chastises Napoleon and predicts his demise, along with a schism in Italy, "astonishing wonders...on the earth and in the air," and the unleashing, in the year 1864, of "a large number of demons...from hell," including Lucifer himself. Then,

> France, Italy, Spain, and England will be at war. Blood will flow in the streets. Frenchman will fight Frenchman, Italian will fight Italian. A general war will follow which will be appalling.... At the first blow of His thundering sword, the mountains and all Nature will tremble in terror, for the disorders and crimes of men have pierced the vault of the heavens. Paris will burn and Marseilles will be engulfed. Several cities will be shaken down and swallowed up by earthquakes. People will believe that all is lost. Nothing will be seen but murder, nothing will be heard but the clash of arms and blasphemy.

According to Melanie's secret, a time of peace would follow and then a series of wars, and then the time of the final clash between the powers of good and evil. Yet,

> [b]efore this comes to pass, there will be a kind of false peace in the world. People will think of nothing but amusement. The wicked will give themselves over to

all kinds of sin. But the children of the holy Church, the children of my faith, my true followers, they will grow in their love for God and in all the virtues most precious to me. Blessed are the souls humbly guided by the Holy Spirit! I shall fight at their side until they reach a fullness of years.

Melanie's secret describes the old world's last days of Armageddon and disaster, natural and man-made, of every kind, before the final cleansing of the Earth and the reunion of God and mankind. After delivering the whole of the secret, Melanie writes of the Lady:

> ...(s)he walked on up to the place where I had gone to see our cows. Her feet touched nothing but the tips of the grass and without bending them. Once on the top of the little mound, the beautiful Lady stopped, and I hurried to stand in front of Her to look at Her so, so closely, and try and see which path she was most inclined to take. For it was all over for me. I had forgotten both my cows and the masters I worked for. I had linked myself forever and unconditionally to my Lady. Yes, I wanted never, never to leave Her. I followed Her with no other motive and fully disposed to serve Her for the rest of my life.

> And thus light took the place of the parts of Her body which were disappearing in front of my eyes; or rather it seemed to me that the body of my Lady was melting into light. Thus the sphere of light rose gently towards the right. I cannot say whether the volume of light decreased as She rose, or whether the growing distance made me see less and less light as

She rose. What I do know, is that I was a long time with my head raised up, staring at the light, even after the light, which kept getting further away and decreasing in volume, had finally disappeared.

Later that day, Melanie and Maximim's masters learn of the event and wonder how to handle the situation; in particular, they worry about how the children will carry out the lady's instructions to bring the messages of warning to the whole world. After much deliberation, it's decided that the two must together meet with the local priest and reveal the entire episode. The local priest of LaSalette was moved to tears by the children's account and immediately preached the messages to his parish congregation. After meeting with the children himself, the mayor of LaSalette also became convinced of the reality and gravity of the episode, and so the wheels were set in motion to bring the messages to the world.

OUR LADY OF LOURDES

Very well-known to people of all faiths are the apparitions at Lourdes, France, which began about 12 years after those at LaSalette, in February of 1858, when a 14-year-old village girl first saw the image of a young woman as she collected firewood with her sisters.

Bernadette Soubirous had been wading through a stream near a grotto, or shrine, near the family's home, when she heard the sound of heavy gusts of wind, but marveled that none of the nearby shrubbery was moving. Attracted by a light in the grotto, Bernadette approached it and saw a girl her own age, wearing a white gown with a blue sash. Her hands held a strand of Rosary beads, and on her feet were yellow roses.

The Sanctuary of Our Lady of Lourdes at Lourdes, France. *(Preacherdoc, Wikimedia Commons.)*

Afraid, Bernadette secretly vowed to keep the vision from her parents, but her sister, Toinette, revealed the incident to their mother. The girls were beaten after the disclosure, yet returned to the grotto several days later.

Upon approaching the site of the first apparition, Bernadette saw the same vision. She had secreted along a vial of holy water in order to discover whether the apparition was a demon in disguise, but when she doused the figure with the liquid, the apparition merely smiled. Following the initial apparitions, word spread quickly through the village, and Bernadette was soon accompanied by growing numbers of curious followers. They watched, fascinated, as Bernadette was seen conversing with an unseen presence and fervently praying, sometimes performing bizarre acts like eating leaves, drinking muddy water, and walking on her knees, kissing the ground. Later, Bernadette would explain that these were acts of humility, performed upon the request of the apparition, to demonstrate her humility and service to the Lord.

During a number of her visits to the grotto, Bernadette was known to go into ecstasy, a state of spiritual rapture during which the stricken person often hears, sees, and feels nothing but the spiritual vision. At times while in ecstasy, Bernadette astounded skeptics, physicians, and other critics by her seemingly supernormal abilities. On one such occasion, a lit candle was held to her hand for 15 minutes without burning her skin.

One day Bernadette was instructed by the apparition to dig for a spring in the ground at the grotto. Clawing through the sandy earth, water at last bubbled up, filthy at first, but eventually running clear. This spring would become a central focus of the apparitions at Lourdes, as the apparition instructed not only Bernadette, but all of the faithful, to drink and bathe in it. Those who did began to find that the waters of the grotto spring seemed to harbor miraculous properties. Many were healed of physical maladies from the mild to the hopeless. Reports spread that broken limbs were healed, internal injuries were instantly repaired, and the terminally ill were restored to youthful vigor.

As might be expected, the activity at the spring soon became a focus of political and social concern, and the grotto area was barricaded in swift time by the local government. It is said that Bernadette herself predicted that the same powers who erected the barricade would pull it down. Indeed, after hearing of the obstruction and the fury against its erection, Napoleon III ordered its removal.

Since the time Bernadette found the well, many millions of pilgrims to Lourdes have drunk the waters of the spring or bathed in it to heal physical and spiritual maladies of every kind. A chemical study of the water was ordered by Mayor Anselme Lacadé of Lourdes in the 1850s, as part of his effort to turn Lourdes into a tourist town that might offer mineral springs as part of the trend toward spa treatments. The water was found to be safe for drinking, but otherwise unexceptional, composed of oxygen, nitrogen, and traces of carbonic acid, lime, iron, potassium, sodium, and other scant minerals. No physical property could explain the incredible claims of its proponents. In the century and a half since Bernadette dug up the spring, 67 cures have been verified as "inexplicable" by the Lourdes Medical Bureau under the incredibly rigorous Vatican standards of medical examination.

Bernadette became a nun, partially to escape the unwanted attention she was receiving as a result of her amazing experiences. She lived a quiet and devoted life before dying at the age of 35 of complications from tuberculosis. Today, her humble behavior in the aftermath of the apparitions is the standard by which all visionaries are judged by the Vatican.

Bernadette was an obvious candidate for canonization, or sainthood, but rigorous criteria had to be met, including healings and miracles, one of which might be incorruption. Incorruption is the failure of the body to decay after death, and the Catholic Church recognizes this phenomena as one miracle to evidence sainthood. Thirty years after her death, Bishop Gauthey of Nevers exhumed the body of Bernadette Soubirous. By his report, backed by supporters of her canonization, several sisters of her order, and two medical doctors, the crucifix and Rosary in Bernadette's hands had both oxidized, but her body was perfectly preserved.

Ten years later, Bernadette's body was exhumed again. A doctor who examined the body reported that it appeared "mummified, covered with patches of mildew" with skin "still present on most parts of the body."

By 1925, canonization seemed imminent, and in that year Bernadette's body was exhumed a third time, but this time for the gathering of relics (typically bone fragments of saints) and the making of a wax mask, which would cover Bernadette's grayish skin and sunken features when her body would be put on permanent display, a not-uncommon practice for the incorruptible.

Today, Bernadette's corpse remains for public viewing, to buoy the faithful and draw in the faithless, in her order's mother house in Nevers. She was canonized in December 1933.

About eight million people a year visit the shrine of Our Lady of Lourdes. In France, the only city with more hotels is Paris.

Our Lady of Fatima

One of the most well-known and influential series of apparitions occurred in Fatima, Portugal, in 1917, and centered around three shepherd children, Lucia Santos, and her cousins, Jacinta and Francisco Marto.

No fewer than four popes of the Roman Catholic Church—Pius XII, John XXIII, Paul VI, and John Paul II—have gone on record to proclaim the apparitions as supernatural in origin. In fact, John Paul II believed Our Lady of Fatima saved him from death by an assassin's bullet in 1981, when he was shot and wounded on the Feast Day of Our Lady of Fatima.

The events began on Sunday afternoon, May 13, 1917, as the children tended sheep in the Cova da Iria, just outside the village. Lucia was the first to experience the vision of a beautiful woman, "brighter than the sun, shedding rays of light clearer and stronger than a crystal ball." This initial apparition led to additional events in the months that followed, in which the woman of light spoke to all three children, urging them to make personal sacrifices for the salvation of sinners. After receiving these messages, the children took to fasting and abstaining from water, tightly cinching their waists with ropes to cause discomfort, and praying nearly constantly. In particular, the children began daily recitation of the Rosary (a special sequence of prayers said on a string of beads), as the woman of light had recommended. During the course of the apparitions, three "secrets" were given to the children, all concerning future world events and punishments, and each hinging on the behavior of humankind, which became known together as the Secrets of Fatima.

That summer, word of the apparitions—which had quickly been accepted as Marian in nature—drew thousands of followers to the region, all of whom trailed behind the children each day as they made their way to the Cova da Iria. In August, a local official decided to put a stop to the "disruptions" and had the children arrested. It is said that, while jailed, they led the other inmates in praying the Rosary.

Fearful that the rumor of "secrets" with political ramifications would cause riots or worse, the official tried many means of interrogation in attempting to extract the secrets from the children; most notably, he threatened to boil them alive in a vat of oil. Despite his most ruthless attempts, the children refused to divulge the contents of the secrets. They resumed their visits to the apparitional site, despite mounting fears of some opponents.

Another point of political tribulation was the question of the coming "miracle." Soon after the apparitions began, talk had circulated about a miraculous event that would coincide with the final apparition, predicted to occur on the October 13, 1917. According to the early message, this miracle would be witnessed by all present at the apparition, and many wondered if the event—or even the fervor of its anticipation—would cause a panic.

On the day in question, an estimated 70,000 people surrounded the children at the Cova da Iria. Rain had poured on the region all morning, finally dissipating to overcastness. The sun was barely visible through the cloud cover, but suddenly Lucia instructed the throng to look to the sky. As they watched, the sun seemed to change colors and spin in the sky. A few saw the blazing sphere "dance" in the heavens.

Some even claimed to see it plunge toward the crowd before returning to its celestial niche. Although witnesses claimed to share in the experience from towns far away, some—even at the Cova—saw nothing.

Reports of the so-called "Miracle of the Sun" covered the newspapers the next morning, chronicling the Sun's "incredible movements outside all cosmic laws" (the popular and respected, squarely anticlerical Portugese paper, *O Seculo*), its appearance of being "loosened from the sky" (the newspaper *Ordem*), and of the crowd "who knelt with outstretched hands...in the presence of a miracle..." (Lisbon daily, *O Dia*.)

The contents of the Three Secrets are believed to have inspired the conversion of many people to Christian and Marian devotion; in particular, the first two Secrets, which paint vivid pictures of Hell (First), and instructions for the salvation of the world from damnation and destruction (Second). The Third Secret was to be revealed after 1960, according to instructions given to Lucia when she received it, but Vatican officials chose to keep it sealed, stating that it would likely never be released to the public. However, in the year 2000, to coincide with the new Millennium of the Church, the Third Secret was announced, revealing a message concerning the death of the pope and other religious leaders. Many, however, believe that part of the Secret—perhaps dealing with world destruction or the collapse of the Church—is still sealed today.

In large part because of the "Miracle of the Sun," Fatima quickly became a point of pilgrimage for thousands of devout believers. Today, as many as a million visitors assemble at Fatima each year in May and October—the months specifically dedicated to Marian devotion, and millions more travel to the site throughout each year.

As for the children themselves, Lucia became a nun and continued to experience apparitions throughout her lifetime. Her cousins, Francisco and Jacinto, both died in the Spanish Flu Epidemic just a few years after the apparitions. Years later, Lucia commented that the Blessed Mother had told the children they would soon die, and that the children willingly and acceptingly shared this news with family members as well as pilgrims during the time of the apparitions. When the children's bodies were exhumed, decades after their deaths, Francisco's corpse had decomposed, but Jacinta's was incorrupt.

THE PROBLEM OF MEDJUGORJE

Not all of the apparitions reported throughout the past century and a half have gone on to prove themselves worthy of approval by the Vatican—at least not yet. An interesting example are the apparitions that took the world by storm as recently as the 1980s.

Since 1981, Christianity—and pro and anticlerical media—has been transfixed on a tiny village in Bosnia-Herzegovina by the name of Medjugorje. Here, each and every day since June of that year, the Blessed Virgin Mary has reportedly been appearing and giving messages to believers and atheists through the channel of six young people ranging in age from 10 to 17: Ivan Dragicevic, Jakov Colo, Marija Pavlovic-Lunetti, Mirjana Dragicevic-Soldo, Vicka Ivankovic-Mijatovic, and Ivanka Ivankovic-Elez. Since the apparitions began nearly 30 years ago, millions of pilgrims and nonbelievers from nearly every nation have visited Medjugorje. They've left with seemingly incredible stories of healing and conversion, reporting supernatural phenomena, emotional renewal, and totally transformed spiritual lives. However, the primary players themselves have led some to believe that the Mejugorjean apparitions are fraudulent at best, diabolical at worst.

In the spring of 2010, the Vatican announced the suspension of the priest who had been the spiritual guide of the Bosnian visionaries from almost the beginning. The charges against him were arguably the worst imaginable. The British *Daily Mail* wrote:

> The Pope has begun a crackdown on the world's largest illicit Catholic shrine—by suspending the priest at the centre of claims that the Virgin Mary has appeared more than 40,000 times. (Pope) Benedict XVI has authorised "severe cautionary and disciplinary measures" against Father Tomislav Vlasic, the former "spiritual director" to six children who said Our Lady was appearing to them at Medjugorje in Bosnia. The Franciscan priest has been suspended after he refused to cooperate into claims of scandalous sexual immorality "aggravated by mystical motivations". He has also been accused of "the diffusion of dubious doctrine, manipulation of consciences, suspected mysticism and disobedience towards legitimately issued orders," and is suspected of heresy and schism. The decree confirming his suspension was signed with the Pope's approval by Cardinal William Levada, head of CDF, and Father Jose Carballo, the

Minister General of the Franciscan Minor Order. It confines Father Vlasic to a Francisan monastery in Italy and bans him from contact with the Queen of Peace community, or with his lawyers without permission from his superior. He is banned from making public appearances, preaching and hearing confessions and he will be required to make a solemn profession of the Catholic faith. The Vatican has warned Father Vlasic that he will be excommunicated if he violates any of the prohibitions.

Adding insult to the injurious claims against the movement's spiritual leader are ongoing charges that the visionaries themselves—as well as the village of Medjugorje—have grown rich from the apparitions, and that the seers and villagers are indulging in lifestyles far different from those that awaited the visionaries of LaSalette, Fatima, and Lourdes. The *Mail* remarked:

> ...(T)he seers have grown wealthy as a result of their claims—and so has their town, which has boomed as a result of the "Madonna gold rush". Some today own smart executive houses with immaculate gardens, double garages and security gates, and one has a tennis court. They also own expensive cars.

Proponents of the Medjugorjean apparitions defend the seers, reminding critics that one of the visionaries of the LaSalette apparitions—a Vatican-approved apparitional phenomenon—died in alcoholic destitution. Are less-than-monastic spiritual lives evidence of fraud or insincerity? Aren't we all tempted by earthly charms?

We may never know how genuine the Medjugorjean apparitions have been. Then again, we just may. According to the Bosnian visionaries, a total of 10 "secrets" will be given to each of the seers before a sequence of three "warnings" that will occur for all the world to witness. Many of these secrets have already been given.

Ten days before each warning, Mirjana alone will receive word of its coming. She will inform the local priest chosen to announce the news to the world. Interestingly, this is not the same priest who was suspended in April 2010. For a week, the two will fast and pray, and on the eighth day the warning will be revealed. According to the seers, the three warnings will make it clear that God is directly intervening in human and earthly events. As a result of the warnings, many will die, and scant time will remain after the first warning for conversion of those who still disbelieve.

7
ANGELS AND DEMONS

GROWING UP BETWEEN HEAVEN AND HELL

A number of years ago, I was at a garden party with some members of our neighborhood garden club, and I was fortunate to meet a woman named Patty who had heard about my research and was anxious to tell me a story about what had happened to her family when her daughters were young.

The two girls were 5 and 7, and the family lived on Chicago's north side in a beautiful, old Victorian home, filled with antiques, including a large Edwardian-era cabinet that stood in the parents' bedroom. On top of the cabinet was a large fishbowl, with a single goldfish swimming inside.

Each year, after Halloween, Patty would put all of the leftover Halloween candy in the top drawer of the cabinet, which was about 5 feet above the ground, out of reach of her daughters' eager hands. The girls, however, knew exactly where it was.

One afternoon in December, Patty was working in the kitchen downstairs as her girls played in their upstairs room. Suddenly, an enormous crash came from the floor above. Patty, terrified, rushed to the stairs. As she passed through the dining room to the steps, as panicked as she was, she stopped suddenly. Inexplicably, a wave of what she described as "peace and tranquility" washed over her. As she stood frozen in place, there appeared a single white feather in the air before her, which drifted past her face and to the ground. The instant it touched the carpet, Patty remembered the crash and bolted upstairs.

The girls were not in their room, and not a sound was to be heard, though she had called to them all the way up the stairs. She found them in her and her husband's bedroom.

The girls were sitting motionless, unharmed, on the windowsill, which in itself was puzzling. The sill was a good 3 feet off the ground, and her littlest one was barely that tall.

Neither of them said a word, but just stared at their mother. The enormous cabinet had fallen over, and was lying against the footboard of the bed, where it had fallen. Sitting in the middle of the bed, with all of the water still inside, was the fishbowl, with the goldfish swimming happily.

The girls never cried. Patty, horrified, asked what had happened.

They had come into the room, the girls said, to get some candy out of the top cabinet drawer. Patty, unaware that this was a habit of theirs, asked how they reached it. What the girls did was to pull out the second drawer from the bottom, and the older child would stand on the edge of it, in order to reach their candy high above. On this particular day, both children had argued over who would procure the candy, and so both of them had climbed up onto the rim of the drawer.

The cabinet began to tip forward from the weight and the fishbowl to slide toward them. The next thing the girls knew, they told Patty, they were sitting on the windowsill and the dresser was lying on its face.

In shock, Patty marveled at what had happened. The enormous dresser should have crushed the girls. She remembered thinking she should have anchored it to the wall when they were babies, as all the warnings said. She hadn't done it because it was an antique and she didn't want to ruin the wood.

Only later, as she washed the dinner dishes, did she remember what had happened on her way upstairs. She remembered the white feather.

Patty's story sounds fantastic, but it is typical of many so-called angelic encounters. In many reports, an unforeseen accident occurs and a blackout period often follows, in which the would-be victim is not conscious of what is happening. Later, all that can be recalled is the incident itself and not the "rescue" from its usually fatal results. Often, a feather makes an appearance to the victim or to a loved one.

Tana Hoy, a medium, talks about white feathers as one sign of angelic visitation, but also believes in other physical signs. Hoy believes that if a person starts to see a lot of pennies around—on the floor, in pockets, in the car—this may be a sign that gifts from Heaven are on the way. She also believes that the dates on the pennies are significant. For example, a penny dated the year of your mother's death may mean she is watching over you. A coin dated the year of your divorce may mean that new and lasting love is on the way. Hoy also believes that angel-shaped clouds are no accident of nature. Indeed, many travelers stranded on desolate roads have reported seeing such clouds and feeling a wash of security and comfort about their plight.

Many "signs" are reportedly sent to us by angels, and not all are in physical form. Audible evidence is plentiful in alleged angelic encounters, and there are ways of differentiating between the real thing and a hallucination or, worse, a demonic visitation.

New Age expert Doreen Virtue presents a clear checklist for validating audio angelic experiences. True angels may be heard as a loud voice outside of ourselves, as if someone is actually in the room with us, or as a quiet voice inside our heart. Interestingly, an angel may also speak to us by repeatedly hearing music in our minds or on the radio, or even opening our ears to someone else's conversation—a conversation that has a message to benefit us.

Doreen Virtue tells us that there are specific critera involved in a true experience: Sentences heard begin with the words "you" or "we." It's obvious that the voice is not coming from yourself. The meaning for your life is overt and immediate. Even dire warnings sound loving and soothing, though danger may be imminent. Celestial music, believe it or not, commonly accompanies the visitation.

The criteria are opposite in the case of false angelic hearing: Sentences begin with the word *I*. The experience feels like the voice is coming from inside the self. The message received is unclear or meaningless. The voice is alarming. Discordant music or loud noises are heard. In these cases, it may be demonic voices, or perhaps voices from one's own subconscience.

WHAT ARE GUARDIAN ANGELS?

The belief that God assigns a guardian to each human soul did not begin with Christianity. The ancient Greeks adopted Plato's belief in the idea, which he likely learned from the ancient religion of Zoroastrianism, though Zoroastrians believe that an individual is free to pick his own guardian from a host of known angels. Angels appear throughout the Christian scriptures, though there is some controversy over whether Guardian Angels only remain with children until the age of accountability, or if they are present throughout adulthood.

No clear catechism demands that Christians believe in Guardian Angels, though much is said in the Christian Scriptures to uphold the theology. The first theologian who wrote about them was Honorius of Autun, who first worked out his theory in the 12th century.

Hierarchy of Angels

Scholastic theologians like Thomas Aquinas classified angels into a definite hierarchy, and most believed that the guardian angels are the low men on the totem pole. (One thinks of the beloved "Clarence" of *It's a Wonderful Life*, the bumbling but well-meaning "Angel, Second Class" sent to save the suicidal George Bailey.)

The First Sphere are the angels who work directly with God: The Seraphim are God's attendants; the Cherubim are protective angels who guarded the road to Eden's Tree of Knowledge; the Thrones are the symbols of Divine justice.

The Second Sphere are the Governors of Heaven: The Dominions are the lords; the Virtues are the overseers of the cosmos; the Powers instill conscience and maintain the flow of history.

The Third Sphere are God's Messengers and Soldiers: The Principalities work with the Powers; the seven Archangels are protectors; the Angels, the lowest rank of all, are most likely to be the guardians of children, as well as those who attend human adults during times of danger or depression.

Interaction With Guardian Angels

As late as 1997, the late Pope John Paul II referred to guardian Angels—twice—in his *Regina Caeli* address, speaking of Catholic followers "supported by our Guardian Angels," suggesting that these beings play a profound role in our spiritual and moral everyday lives.

A guardian angel escorts her charges through the dangers of a stormy night. *(Artist unknown.)*

Indeed, both Christian mystics and modern psychic mediums have reported extensive and intermittent dialogue with their Guardian Angels. As a girl, Saint Gemma Galgani, an Italian Christian mystic of the late 19th century, claimed to have had long discussions with her guardian angel, who showed the girl deep insights into prayers and the psalms, and who, according to Galgani, taught her appropriate behavior as well.

Even the unborn are believed by Christians to benefit from a special guardian's influence. As explicitly stated in the Apocalypse of Peter: "Aborted infants are entrusted to a guardian angel, so that having obtained a share in the gnosis they may arrive at a better destiny."

In Chicago, each morning and evening, children all over the city invoke their guardians with a prayer taught in their earliest days. Whether our own private angels remain with us into adulthood or not, an overwhelming number say it until their dying day:

Angel of God, my guardian dear

To whom God's love commits me here.

Ever this day be at my side

To light, to guard, to rule and guide. Amen.

Demons

In February 2008, newspapers around the world picked up on a bizarre incident that took place in Kampala, Uganda, in which more than 100 schoolchildren were reported to have been possessed by demons. The local *New Vision* newspaper reported that the school's headmaster had described the students as "hysterical...totally mad...chasing everybody... throwing stones, banging doors and windows." Incredibly, a similar event had occurred a year earlier, that time affecting twice as many children. It was believed by many that the incidents could be traced to a "spell" that was put on the school by four local residents.

The scientific-minded will quickly dismiss these events as mass hysteria, bacteria in the water supply, or perhaps drugs in the lunch trays, thanks to disgruntled school employees; however, belief in demons—unclean, evil spirits— runs through all major religions, and the fear of them stems from the widespread belief that they can possess animals and humans. Children, it is believed, are especially prone to demonic possession because of their purity and lack of spiritual development or self-protection.

Christian scripture teaches that demons are fallen angels who became followers of Lucifer after he was banished from Heaven. Incorrectly, some believe that demons are the Hellish equivalent of saints: souls who once walked the Earth as humans and now have a "special place in Hell," so to speak, and assist the Devil in influencing humans toward evil thoughts and actions. In fact, according to Christian theology, demons—like angels—were never human.

Classifications of Demons

Like Angels, there is a hierarchical structure for demons. There is less of a class system, however, the classifications denote their various methods or who they target. There are a number of such systems, but one of the first was conceived of by Alphonso de Spina, a Spanish bishop, in the mid-15th century. He writes of goblins, incubi and succubi, familiars, and demons whose special mission is to torment the saints.

Demons' work entirely consists of tempting human beings into sin; in particular, they toil incessantly to undermine faith in God. It is believed that demons have a particular penchant for children because they have little spiritual armor developed and are ready to be shaped for sin. Demons also are believed to simply enjoy instilling fear, and pick the easiest victims to shake up.

POSSESSION AND ITS REMEDIES

If a person or animal is possessed by a demon, relief may come by deliverance or exorcism. A deliverance may be performed by any baptized Christian and may aid a mild case of possession; for example, one in which the demon is believed to have caused a substance addiction or an emotional or spiritual illness, such as depression or anxiety. Oftentimes, as previously discussed, dabbling in the occult or even moving into an ostensibly haunted home can begin the process of possession, but if the change in the victim is noticed early on, deliverance may do the trick. However, if possession has progressed to an advanced stage, exorcism is believed to be the victim's only hope.

Though many Christian denominations practice rites of exorcism, the granddaddy of them all is that of the Roman Catholic Church, arguably the most regimented and intense of all exorcism rites. In the church today, when a case comes to light, mental or other bodily illness is assumed, and only after the failure of rigorous examinations and traditional medical treatments can the exorcism be sanctioned. Before the sanction, the case must be found to conform to strict criteria that may include the following symptoms: speaking foreign or ancient languages of which the possessed has no prior knowledge; supernatural abilities and strength; knowledge of hidden or remote things that the possessed has no way of knowing; an aversion to anything holy; and profuse blasphemy or sacrilege. The exorcist—one of a scarce and elite class of ordained priests—must undergo a strict period of preparation for the rite, including rigorous fasting and prayer, as the performance of the ritual places the exorcist and victim in extreme spiritual and physical danger.

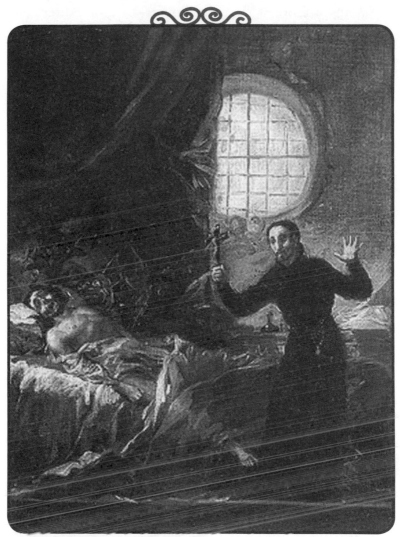

St. Francis Borgia performing an exorcism, as portrayed by the artist Goya. *(Photograph, Wikimedia Commons.)*

Without a doubt the most famous case of exorcism—outside the New Testament—remains that of little "Robbie Doe," the Maryland boy whose bizarre story became the basis for the hugely popular book and film *The Exorcist*. As is the case with numerous reports of "demonic" activity, the maladies of this young boy commenced, it seems, with a Ouija board.

Beginning in 1949, the adolescent Robbie and his family began to experience bizarre occurrences in their Cottage City, Maryland, home, beginning with scratching sounds that seemed to come from inside the walls and ceilings of the house. Believing that mice had gotten in, the family called an exterminator, who found nothing. Later, footsteps were heard, and objects were found to have moved around the house. It wasn't long before Robbie himself became the focus of the phenomena. His bed began to shake at night, and invisible hands repeatedly pulled his bedding off his body.

Experts later believed that the events may have begun with the death of Robbie's Aunt Tillie. Tillie had been a practicing Spiritualist in life—someone whose religion is based on communication with the dead. She had taught Robbie to use a Ouija board to communicate with spirits and, as mentioned earlier, many opponents of the Ouija believe that the board is one of the quickest ways to demonic possession.

The Reverend Luther Schulze, the pastor of the family's Lutheran church, came to pray with Robbie, but the prayers didn't affect the phenomena. Schulze decided to conduct an experiment to determine whether Robbie or his house was the cause of the disturbances. He invited Robbie to spend the night in the rectory of the church to see if the phenomena would be repeated there.

The night Robbie stayed, the reverend's wife went to sleep in the guest room, and Robbie and the pastor in the twin beds located in the couple's room. Almost immediately after the lights were turned off, Schulze heard Robbie's bed begin to shake, and, not longer after, mysterious scratching sounds began in the walls. The pastor's prayers seemed to only intensify the activity, so Schulze helped Robbie out of the shaking bed and into an armchair instead. It wasn't long, however, before the chair began to move, sliding back and forth before crashing itself into a wall. After a moment, it dumped Robbie onto the floor.

After the events at the rectory, Schulze didn't know what to think. He sent Robbie's parents to a doctor and for counseling, and he wrote to pioneering parapsychologist J. B. Rhine, who had founded the world's first parapsychology laboratory at Duke University. Robbie checked out fine with the medical doctors and, although no phenomena occurred in the presence of J.B. and Louisa Rhine, the latter believed that the reported activity was very much in line with other poltergeist cases he had studied.

Things seemed hopeful, as Rhine convinced Schulze that the activity was likely coming from the boy's own displaced energy, but something then happened that turned the situation dire: Bloody scratches began to appear on Robbie's torso, causing the family much alarm. It was then that they decided to ask the Roman Catholic Church to investigate.

Inquiring for help at the nearby Catholic church, a priest named Edward Hughes advised the family to bless the rooms with holy water and to light blessed candles. After blessing the house, Robbie's mother put the bottle on a shelf, but it flew off at once with violent force, but did not break.

Some reports talk about several attempts to baptize Robbie as a Catholic: once while Robbie was hospitalized during the early disturbances, and a second time at a local church. One account claims that, as Robbie's uncle drove him to the church for the sacrament, Robbie grabbed his throat and screamed, "You son of a bitch, you think I'm going to be baptized, but you are going to be fooled!" The baptism, normally a ritual of less than 20 minutes, was said to have lasted almost three hours, as the boy went into violent fits when he was asked to renounce Satan.

After Robbie was discharged from the hospital, his mother took him to St. Louis, where she had grown up, hoping that a change of scenery might break the "spell" on Robbie. Before the trip, the bloody word *LOUIS* was found scratched into Robbie's skin.

In St. Louis, the disturbances continued. Robbie's extended family also witnessed the scratches appearing on Robbie's flesh, and objects moved as they had at home in Maryland. The family appealed to a local Catholic church to send someone to the house. When he arrived, he blessed Robbie's room and his bed, but throughout the blessing the bed shook violently and new scratches appeared on Robbie's skin. After witnessing these events, the priest agreed to return the next night. When he did, he brought along Father William Bowdern, who—after much effort and anguish—was to become Robbie's exorcist.

While the two priests were in the home, nothing happened, but the moment they left, a thundering crash was heard. All rushed into Robbie's room to find that an enormous bookcase had spun around, a chair had flown across the room, and a crucifix under Robbie's pillow had shot to the footboard of the bed.

After these incidents, the priests requested permission from their bishop to perform the rite of exorcism. William Bowdern was given the commission, and the ritual began in the rectory of nearby St. Frances Xavier Church. The ritual went on for days, and after a time the decision was made to move Robbie to the Alexian Brothers Hospital, as reportedly his medical needs and violent behavior were too straining on the rectory quarters.

During the many repetitions of the rite over many months, Robbie reportedly spoke in Latin and Aramaic, blasphemed and swore at the top of his lungs, and engaged in spitting, projectile vomiting, urinating on and slapping the priests in attendance. His body was seen to contort into pretzel-like shapes, and once he reportedly flew across the room at Fr. Bowdern. During this incident, witnesses claimed that when Robbie's hands hit the ritual book it dissolved into a million pieces, which fell to the floor like confetti.

Bowdern was overwhelmed. Dozens of recitations of the exorcism rite had seemed to only worsen Robbie's condition. He decided to take Robbie back to Maryland and continue the exorcism at home. During the train ride, Robbie reportedly punched Fr. Bowdern in the testicles and laughed, "That's a nutcracker for you!"

In Maryland, no church or hospital would provide a place for the exorcism, so Robbie and Bowdern returned to St. Louis, where the exorcist began fervently rehashing old cases that had succeeded. Armed with new energy—and with Robbie's wrists bound with religious medals and a crucifix in hand—Bowdern resumed the ritual.

It is said that during that April night in 1949, five attendants held Robbie down as Bowdern relentlessly repeated the exorcism rite, demanding that the demon identify itself. Robbie raged and spat and screamed, blaspheming and cursing without rest. Finally, toward morning, he cried out that he was a fallen angel. Almost at once, a deep, male voice identified itself as St. Michael the Archangel, the angel known for battling the Devil. Robbie quieted completely, opened his eyes, smiled, and fell asleep. The ordeal was over.

The Catholic Church later filed a full report stating that the case had been that of a "genuine demonic possession." Father John Nicola, the religious advisor to the film *The Exorcist*, reported that more than 40 people had signed an affidavit swearing that they had witnessed paranormal phenomena in the case of "Robbie Doe."

After the exorcism, Robbie Doe attended Catholic high school and went on to raise a family. He has had no further recurrences; in fact, he has had no other supernatural experiences at all. To this day, Robbie's identity remains a secret. The few researchers who have done the extensive work to track him down have come to protect his privacy in the end. It is reported that his best childhood friend, still in contact, has never even told his wife.

Father Gabriele Amorth, 85, has held the position of chief exorcist for the Vatican for almost three decades and has performed the ritual in more than 70,000 cases of demonic possession. Fr. Amorth went on record as approving the case in the *Exorcist* film, stating that, despite Hollywood effects, it related a "substantially exact" case of true possession, in which extreme and inexplicable phenomena are to be expected. Indeed, Amorth reports that, in some of the true cases, it has taken more than a half dozen assistants to restrain the victim during the rite, and that, during the ritual, victims have been known to spit out nails and glass.

The debate over whether supernatural beings—good and evil—actually influence our lives is one that has continued throughout the modern age—and survived. Today, when we speak of "demons," we are most likely talking about neurological influences on our thoughts and behaviors. When we talk of angels, we are usually referring to benevolent friends, family members, and associates who go the extra mile to make life better or work easier, or who have a knack for resolving problems. But angels and demons of the very supernatural variety are still credited with some of the most disturbing events of people's lives. When we credit an angel for plucking us from the jaws of bodily death—or blame a demon for landing a child in a mental institution—are we really as "behind the times" as some believe? Or is there truly a spiritual battle quietly raging just below the service of our thoroughly modern lives?

8

THE POWER OF THE POLTERGEIST

In his essay, "Ghosts and Liminality," parapsychologist George Hansen observed of liminal—or transitional—experiences: "Liminal phenomena are typically transient, ephemeral, and have an affinity for chaos, transition, and instability. They are also usually viewed as slightly disreputable."

Certainly this definition perfectly fits one of the most controversial and disturbing case bodies in parapsychology: that of *poltergeist* phenomena. Indeed, the definition suits even more perfectly the typical poltergeist *agent*. In a poltergeist case, the agent is the individual—usually an adolescent—around whom the paranormal activity seems to revolve. The activity is typically of an intensely physical variety. Poltergeists were long believed—and still are by many—to be the spirits of the dead. The word is the German for "noisy ghost," and poltergeist infestations are marked by doors opening and closing, unexplained knocks, disembodied voices, and sourceless music, the movement and teleportation of objects, and family members—especially the agent—being pushed out of bed or down the stairs, having their hair pulled, and being punched, kicked, or bitten. Commonly and unfortunately, the poltergeist agent, though first seemingly innocent, resorts to fraudulent production of the phenomena, in order to please spectators, draw attention, or prove that the activity is genuine. As a result, incredible controversy has always accompanied these enigmatic manifestations.

In 1984, Tina Resch was a 14-year-old former foster child living in the Columbus, Ohio, home of adoptive parents who were increasingly troubled by her rebellious behavior. That year, inexplicable phenomena began in the home that, in short time, attracted the attention of local news media and, later, the scrutiny of arguably the world's most knowledgeable researcher of poltergeist activity, William Roll.

Tina Resch was left at the hospital by her mother just 10 months after birth. The next day, she was placed in foster care, where her future parents had cared for more than 250 foster children in the past. Attending primary school, Tina found herself constantly in trouble, charged with throwing pencils and erasers, and otherwise disrupting classes. Later, her mother would recall that no one—students or teachers—ever actually saw Tina touching these objects, and so some wonder if her alleged telekenetic abilities had manifested at a much younger age.

The disturbances in school—deliberate or not—isolated Tina from her classmates. She was diagnosed as "hyperactive" and much show was made by teachers of administering her medication during class each day. Eventually, peer ridicule grew to violence when Tina's classmates literally tied her up on the playground, taunting her as she cried.

Tina was removed from school, and her parents hired a tutor to school her. In between study sessions, Tina helped care for the numerous foster children in the Resch home, a situation that she seemed to enjoy. But one day, the Resch's world turned upside-down again, this time, far worse.

From the first day, the unusual physical activity in the home was full-throttle, beginning with electrical and numerous malfunctions of the lights, microwave oven, kitchen clock, and television, and leading to extremely bizarre and inexplicable manifestions, including one incident where eggs stored in the Resch's refrigerator shot through the *closed* refrigerator door, breaking on the kitchen floor.

Media focus on this apparently large scale case of Recurrent Spontaneous Psychokinesis (RSPK) resulted in the capture of a number of infamous photographs believed by many to be truly paranormal. In particular, photojournalist

Fred Shannon of *The Columbus Dispatch* snapped a shot of Tina sitting in an armchair with a telephone handset and its coiled cable propelling itself across her body from the phone cradle on the side table. The now-famous "flying phone photo" has been published countless times by proponents and skeptics alike. However, the photo and the testimonies of a social worker, Tina's foster parents, and the photographer himself were undermined by later events. Namely, as the case progressed and attention swelled, Tina was caught faking phenomenon, giving the explanation that she was tired and simply wanted everyone to go home and leave her alone.

Parapsychologist William Roll visited the Resch home in March 1994, having been informed of the case by the Rhine Research Center, the academic descendent of Duke University's original parapsychology laboratory. *The Columbus Dispatch* had contacted the Center after Fred Shannon's story and photos ran, and Roll later admitted that, when he agreed to visit the Resch home, he expected to find nothing more than a teenager craving attention.

What that first visit led to, instead, was an eight-year investigation of Tina Resch by Roll, who went on to pen an entire book on the case, *Unleashed,* published in 2004, 20 years after the start of the events. Roll also analyzed the case for the popular paranormal magazine *Fortean Times,* recalling the steps he had taken to diagnose Tina's troubles and arrive at a workable theory about what lay at the heart of the incredible phenomena:

The famous "flying phone" photograph of Tina Resch, as captured by photojournalist Fred Shannon during a visit to the Resch home. (*Photograph, Wikimedia Commons.*)

To establish or eliminate the possibility that Tina suffered complex partial seizures (CPS), I suggested to the Resches that they take her to a neurologist. They did so in March—before my arrival—with a follow-up in May. John Corrigan reported that her brain-wave record showed no epileptic spikes, but the tests demonstrated occasional muscle jerks, blinking, twisting, and incessant finger movements.

The results of Tina's neurological examination were analyzed extensively. It was suggested that Tina may have suffered from a mild form of Tourette's syndrome:

Tina had an urge to express herself that she could not suppress. At home with Joan this often caused her to be "loud" and brought on demands for quiet, which released torrents of loud and foul language. This would lead to a slap on the face, or when Tina became too big for Joan to handle, a beating from John. Verbal explosions and at least one physical attack on Joan were her ways of dealing with being rebuffed. Tina's urge to express herself even in the face of punishment was consistent with (the) diagnosis and was one of the pieces in the puzzle of her RSPK. We also discovered other signs that there might be an anomaly in Tina's brain stem, which is associated with day/night functions and the parasympathetic system. When Tina had her third neurological examination in May 1984, she mentioned frequent aches at the back of her head during the day; she also described persistent coldness and spells of daydreaming. Her left eyelid twitched, and she was less sensitive on the left side of her body. This idea was explored further during Tina's visit to Durham in October 1984, where Steve Baumann of the University of North Carolina tested for anomalies in her upper brain stem. The results indicated a faster than usual stream of electrical impulses in the pons region. The night before the occurrences began, she had a fight with her father which may have brought the stress to the breaking point. Tina's brain was already susceptible to Tourette-type discharges, and she had a brainstem anomaly that may have increased these discharges and focused them on significant objects.

Finally, a geomagnetic storm may have tipped the scales. The puzzle behind Tina's psychokinesis was beginning to fall together and make sense to me. Now all that remained was what it would mean to Tina.

In 1992, Tina Resch (now Boyer) was a divorced mother of a 3-year-old girl named Amber. That year, she was jailed, along with her boyfriend, David Herrin, for the murder of her baby daughter.

The chain of events leading up to Amber's death began when Tina was only 16. According to reports, Tina's parents decided to sell their home in 1986, due to the disfavor of neighbors after their daughter's publicity. They apparently informed Tina that she would have to find somewhere else to live, that she would not be welcome to live in their new home. A minor, Tina faced the choice of either marrying her boyfriend or living in a juvenile detention center. Horrified, she disappeared and announced that she and her boyfriend had eloped. Though this wasn't true, the couple later married, but her husband became abusive as well, and Tina divorced him, later becoming pregnant by an anonymous father. For the baby's well-being, Tina married boyfriend Larry Boyer, who also beat her, eventually into unconsciousness. After divorcing Boyer, Tina went to live with the Rolls and seemed ready to turn around her ill-fated life. She began nursing and computer courses and, some time later, met David Herrin.

At the time of the toddler's death, Tina was at the home of a friend who was helping Tina write an account of the mysterious events of her earlier life. Herrin was the only one in the home with the child. It was later discovered that Amber had been sodomized, and Tina passed a polygraph test with flying colors. Nonetheless, Tina was jailed and awaited trial for two and a half years. In October 1994, she accepted a plea bargain to avoid the possibility of capital punishment. Tina was sentenced to life plus 20 years in prison. Her boyfriend received 20 years for cruelty to children, with the possibility of parole.

Interestingly, Tina had spoken many times with Roll about feeling incapable of expressing her feelings, even in the face of turmoil or abuse. When she would speak her mind or become upset, she was reportedly severely beaten by her adoptive father. She was also allegedly molested by her brother. Her best friend died in a car accident at the age of 14, a loss that she kept inside, expressing little grief at the time.

Is it possible that Tina's unsettled physiological makeup—diagnosed early on as hyperactivity and, later, as Tourette's syndrome—led to the many difficult and, eventually, tragic circumstances of her life? Is it also possible that Tina plea bargained in the face of her murder charge because she was used to being disbelieved regarding her actions, just as she had been from her earliest days at school?

Though first believed to be the result of fun-loving or malevolent, highly active spirits, poltergeist activity has survived the scrutiny of many modern scientists, who have come to believe that the phenomena *are* real—but decidedly *un-*spirited. In the laboratory, attempts to re-create the dramatic effects of poltergeist cases have failed; however, experts are convinced this is because the phenomena only occur within the complex dynamic of the family situation. Undaunted by skeptics who cry "fraud" in the face of the often bizarre cases that continue to come to light, parapsychologists like the late William Roll have tirelessly labored to convince science that the power of the mind can be a truly dangerous thing, leaving in its wake physical and familial havoc, lasting emotional trauma, and—in at least one case—death.

9

FUN AND GAMES

HAUNTED TOYS

A handful of years ago I was searching for something on the Internet auction site, eBay, and came across a selection of wares under the category "haunted items." Intrigued, I opened the list and found an interesting assortment of jewelry, furniture, mirrors, paintings, and—fascinatingly—toys. Most prevalent were so-called haunted dolls, especially porcelain or china ones, whose owners claimed that they moved from room to room, talked, or even brought bad luck upon their owners.

My eye fixed on one listing in particular, too bizarre to avoid: a haunted, talking Pee Wee Herman doll with a pull string. The seller, a single mom from some little town somewhere in Middle America, had moved with her small son into a crumbling old home and had found the doll in a trunk of toys in the basement. Her son immediately grabbed it and refused to give it up, so she let him play with it, though the "talking" function no longer worked. But although the doll and the boy were at first inseparable, it wasn't long before the son began trying to throw the doll away. When questioned about these attempts, he claimed that "the bad man" was bothering him. Further questioning revealed that this "bad man" seemed to be an entity attached to the doll itself, and that despite attempts to throw away the doll, it always reappeared in the boy's room, along with the unwanted presence of the "bad man." Against my better judgment, I bid on the doll and won it. By the time the package arrived, I had worked myself up into quite a frenzy over it. My own daughters were quite small at the time, and I wondered if anything untoward would ensue.

After about two weeks, absolutely nothing frightening had happened, except that the doll's pull string was broken, so when pulled, Pee Wee would drawl a string of gurgly, masculine-toned jibberish, vaguely evocative of a scene or two from *The Exorcist*. I considered sending the doll to demonologist John Zaffis—nephew of the legendary, late "demon hunter" Ed Warren—who collects (and "binds" or spiritually de-activates) such evil objects for his museum of haunted objects on the East Coast. I ended up deciding, however, that Pee Wee probably wasn't worth the postage. I decided to throw him out, reasoning that, if he mysteriously returned, I would ship him away for Zaffis to deal with.

Although my allegedly haunted doll wasn't all it was advertised to be, not so with some others that have made their less-than-cuddly mark on the lives of their owners. John Zaffis's inspiration to collect paranormal objects comes from his famous uncle and aunt—demonologists Ed and Lorraine Warren—who founded the nation's first museum of haunted objects: the Warren Occult Museum in Connecticut. There, still today, lives one of the nastiest dolls on record: the evil and infamous Annabelle.

Annabelle is an oversized Raggedy Ann doll who belonged to a young Hartford nurse named Donna. Donna's mother gave her the doll as a novel birthday present, but not long after, the doll seemed to start moving through the apartment by itself. Ed and Lorraine Warren document the case on their Web archives (*edandlorrainewarren.com*), sharing the chilling details of one of their most talked-about cases.

Donna and her roommate, Angie, first noticed the strange activity when they'd arrive home from work to find the doll in a place where it hadn't been left. Each morning, after making her bed, Donna would place the doll in the middle, with its arms out to the sides and its legs straight in front, against the pillows. However, when the nurse would return in the evening, she would find the doll's arms or legs crossed

Legendary paranormal researcher Lorraine Warren holds the evil Annabelle the doll. *(Photograph courtesy of Lorraine Warren and Tony Spera.)*

or folded, in a number of different positions. When Donna started deliberately changing the doll's morning position to see if it was really moving, she would come home at night to find the position had, indeed, been altered.

As time went on, the doll became more active. Though it was always left on Donna's bed in the morning, the young women would come home to find the doll sitting on the living room sofa. Once, they found the doll kneeling on the living room floor, though when the girls themselves tried to get the doll to kneel, it flopped over.

Even more chilling were the messages the doll would leave. Incredibly, the women began to find notes around the house, written in pencil, on parchment paper, in a child's handwriting. The notes insisted, "Help Us" or "Help Lou." Angie's boyfriend and the girls swore there was not even a pencil in the house, let alone parchment paper. After the notes began, the nurses became convinced that someone was coming into the locked apartment and playing pranks, so they began to rig the apartment in order to validate their theory. They taped the windows and doors and even rearranged rugs so that an obvious trace would be left by the intruder, but nothing was ever disturbed.

Things with Annabelle turned sinister one evening when the women returned from work to find what looked like blood on the back of Annabelle's hand—and three drops of the same substance on her dress. This event led the roommates to believe that the apartment or the doll was haunted, and they contacted a medium to try to communicate with the spirit in question.

> We learned that a little girl died on this property, Donna told the Warrens. She was seven years old and her name was Annabelle Higgins. The Annabelle spirit said she played in the fields long ago before these apartments were built. They were happy times for her, she told us. Because everyone around here was grown-up, and only concerned with their jobs, there was no one she could relate to, except us. Annabelle felt that we would be able to understand her. That's why she began moving the rag doll. All Annabelle wanted was to be loved, and so she asked if she could stay with us and move into the doll. What could we do? So we said yes.

Ed and Lorraine Warren eventually flew to the young women's apartment to investigate the case, which, according to the Warrens, was not a haunting at all, but a case of full-blown demonic possession. The Warrens believed that the demon had used the story of Annabelle to pull at the young nurses' heartstrings to gain entry into the doll and, ultimately, their lives and minds.

Angie's boyfriend, Lou, claimed that Annabelle had "gotten into his head," so to speak, long before, and that he was plagued by bad dreams in which the doll tried to strangle him. The dreams came to bizarre fruition some time later. Lou remembered:

> It was about ten or eleven o'clock at night, and we were reading over maps because I was going off on a trip the next day. Everything was quiet at the time. Suddenly, we both heard sounds in Donna's room that made us think that someone had broken into the apartment. I quietly got up and tip-toed to the bedroom door, which was closed. I waited until the noises stopped, then I carefully opened the door and reached in and switched on the light. Nobody was in there! Except, the Annabelle doll was tossed on the floor in a corner. I went in alone and walked over to the thing to see if anything unusual had happened. But as I got close to the doll, I got the distinct impression that somebody was behind me.

When Lou spun around, he suddenly screamed and clutched his chest. Upon reaching him, Angie found his shirt covered in blood and, underneath, a series of deep scratch marks—almost like burns—on his chest.

After the attack on Lou, Donna sought help from an Episcopalian priest who, though startled by the story, believed the young people's reports and contacted a second priest who had extensive knowledge of spirit possession. The

Warrens asked Donna to have this priest join them in the apartment, to perform a simple exorcism, convinced that the active nature of the phenomena indicated that it was demonic in origin and that, given a bit more time, the three young people would have been seriously injured or even killed.

When the priest arrived, Ed Warren explained his theory about the events and convinced the priest to recite the exorcism prayers and to bless Donna, Angie, and Lou. Afterward, Lorraine Warren—a prominent clairvoyant—declared that the home and the young people were free of the demon. To ensure that Annabelle would no longer be a problem, the Warrens took her with them when they returned to their home in Massachussetts. As a precaution, Ed placed the doll in the back seat of the car and elected to drive home on surface roads rather than at the high speeds of the interstate, just in case.

Sure enough, it wasn't long into their journey that the brakes and steering of their nearly new car began to malfunction. After several close calls with disaster, Ed pulled over and dowsed the doll with holy water. No further incidents occurred on that trip.

Clearly, however, the spirit had not been fully separated from the doll. When the Warrens reached home, Ed placed Annabelle in his home office, sitting in a chair beside his desk. On several occasions, Ed claimed the doll had levitated or risen off the chair on its own, and that it soon began moving from room to room, as it had done in Donna and Angie's apartment. Eventually, the Warrens placed Annabelle in their Occult Museum in Monroe, Connecticut, in a glass case covered with warnings about the doll's malevolence.

Some have not heeded the warnings, however. The museum staff recalls one afternoon when a young man visited the museum with his girlfriend and, during a tour, went up to Annabelle's case, rapped on the glass, and taunted the doll, urging the entity to attack him. Ed removed the young man from the museum. An hour or so later, the young man crashed his motorcycle, dying in the accident. His girlfriend lived to tell that the last thing he did before suddenly veering fatally into a tree was to make a joke about Annabelle.

Much less physically attractive than Annabelle—but just as paranormally enticing—is the internationally renowned doll known as Robert. Robert the Doll is a truly dreadful, handmade thing, vaguely resembling a boy in a sailor suit. It was given to Robert Eugene ("Gene") Otto, a boy from an affluent Key West family, by the family's Caribbean maid. It is said that when the maid was angrily dismissed by Gene's mother, the doll began to take on a life of its own.

Robert—christened with the first name of its owner—went everywhere with little Gene, even sitting next to him in his own chair at mealtimes. Nothing odd at first, perhaps, for a little boy and his favorite toy, but soon the attachment grew sinister. Years later, the Ottos' servants reported hearing conversations—in two distinct voices—coming from Gene's room from those earliest days. During these conversations, Gene's voice would sound frightened or nervous, and the other voice demanding and terse. Sometimes, the exchanges were so disturbing that the servants alerted Gene's mother, who would rush to the scene, only to find Gene curled up in a corner, with Robert above him, in a chair or on a table, staring at the child.

Soon, as in the case of Annabelle, the activity escalated, moving from the little owner's bedroom throughout the house. Paranormal activity erupted, leaving in its trail broken dishes, torn bedclothes, and toys twisted and seemingly smashed against the wall. Famously, when Gene was accused of it all, he promptly protested, "Robert did it!"

The activity in the house became so pronounced that Robert's great aunt, during a visit, told servants to take Robert from Gene and store the doll in the attic of the house. She died in her sleep the next night, after which Robert was mysteriously found in Gene's room again, though no one ever admitted to bringing him down.

Gene grew up, but not out of his obsession with Robert, and soon all of Key West knew about the strange relationship the two shared. In short order, local children spread stories heard from the servants at the Otto house: stories of unusual events far beyond the odd relationship between doll and owner. When Gene's parents died, Gene moved into the master bedroom, and Robert inherited his owner's room— the infamous "Turret Room" in the corner of the house.

Gene and Robert lived alone in the house for years, with a bare staff of two to cook meals and do odd jobs. Further staff would not remain, and Gene grew lonely. He finally married, but trouble plagued the union from day one, as Gene still demanded the constant companionship of Robert, who took all of the couple's meals with them and even slept in their bedroom. All we know of the fate of Gene's wife is that she went quickly mad and died.

Gene himself died soon after, and Robert was found by the eventual new tenants in an attic trunk. According to legend, Robert freely roamed the house during the new tenancy, until one night he was found at the foot of the new master's bed, holding a butcher knife. This was, finally, Robert's last stand in his owner's home. He was given into the care of the East Martello Museum, a historical collection in Key West, where he remains today.

Both at the museum and back home in the Otto house, Robert is said to be very much present indeed. At East Martello, visitors have a hard time snapping photographs of Robert, as frames typically turn out blank—if the camera batteries don't die first. Some tourists claim that Robert's facial expression has changed from smiling to grimacing right before their eyes. And at the Otto home (now the popular "Artist's House" bed and breakfast), Robert's famous giggling and destructive habits continue, rendering "Robert did it!" a phrase that still rings through the halls.

OUIJA TROUBLE

The Ouija board, a highly controversial "toy," is today still manufactured and distributed by Parker Brothers, but the idea of a "talking board" or "spirit board" is an ancient one, and its many manifestations have had the same basic makeup. A flat rectangular board is covered with the letters of the alphabet, numbers from one to nine (as well as zero), and the words *yes, no, hello,* and *goodbye.* Players or "sitters" place the tips of their fingers on a planchette—a small, pointer-shaped piece of wood or plastic set on the board. Sitters ask questions of the board and are sometimes rewarded with answers, as the planchette moves around the board to spell out words and dates, ostensibly with the aid of spirits.

Possibly the first mention of Ouija-type usage appears in the historical records of the Song Dynasty of China, around 1100 BC. Documents refer to *fuji* or "planchette writing" as a tool for communicating with the dead. In fact, some of the scriptures of the Daozang were reportedly produced by planchette writing.

A board was not used in planchette writing until the mid-1800s, and attended the rise of the Spiritualist movement, which began in New York State in 1848. In that year, in a little home in Hydesville, the Fox sisters began communicating with an alleged spirit in their home, asking the spirit to rap on the walls to answer their questions "yes" or "no" and to indicate dates and letters by series of raps, much like Morse code.

Spiritualism—the religion of communicating with the dead through seances and mediumship—became a widespread movement in the late 19th century, and many new methods were developed to facilitate communication with the other side. Entrepreneurs Elijah Bond and Charles Kennard were the first to request a patent for a planchette and an alphabet board. They received U.S. Patent No. 446, 054 in 1891. Subsequently, one of Kennard's employers—William Fuld—assumed the manufacture of the boards. In 1901, he started making his own boards, sold under the name Ouija. Fuld died in 1927, but his company continued to manufacture the boards until 1966, when Fuld's family sold the business to Parker Brothers.

Increasingly, Ouija boards are believed by many to be very dangerous tools indeed, and hardly the "toys" or "games" they are advertised to be. Books, films, documentaries, and the Internet all carry the common message against them, a great number based on allegedly true accounts. Essentially, opponents of the board believe that the boards open up communication with demonic entities, and that the "loved ones" or spirits of the dead who identify themselves during Ouija board sessions are actually non-human entities engaging in trickery. Warnings against the use of the board became widespread beginning in the 1920s, when a number of prominent mental health experts publicly called Ouija boards a "dangerous factor in unbalancing the mind" (Dr. Curry) and warned against "the serious problem of alienation and mental derangement attending ignorant psychic experiments" (Dr. Carl Wickland).

Probably the most famous report of a demon being summoned by a Ouija board is that of the young Maryland boy who became the inspiration for the novel *The Exorcist* (see Chapter 7). Though accounts differ as to whether or not Robbie Doe actually used a Ouija board before the events began—as is portrayed in the book and film—it is certain that he was dabbling in communication with the dead with his aunt, a practicing Spiritualist. Although skeptics of the case have suggested that Robbie was mentally ill, none can explain how the illness simply vanished after the series of exorcisms he endured over the course of many months.

Natasha Cornett, the Kentucky teenager who was convicted of murdering a family at a roadside rest stop in 1997, was allegedly heavily involved in occult and Satanic culture. Along with her six "followers," she frequently engaged in Ouija board usage, leading many critics to further slam the use of such boards.

Of course, skeptics offer simple explanations for the effects that occur during Ouija sessions—and the bizarre behavior that sometimes results. The skeptics' explanation for the movement of the planchette is the so-called "ideomotor effect." Ideomotor action is the subconscious influence of the mind on motor activity. In the case of the Ouija, the minds of the players or sitters subtly and unconsciously influence the muscles in their fingers to imperceptibly move the planchette. The term *ideomotor* itself hails from the earliest days of Modern Spiritualism, when William Carpenter tried to explain the success of dowsers finding water using two sticks and the phenomenon of Spiritualist mediums making tables move during seances.

Some psychologists believe that, once the ball is rolling and the unconscious mind starts "causing" the sitters, through the board, to invent stories and scenarios, almost anything is possible, including the bizarre and frightening phenomena that are often reported.

The first Ouija-reported incident I learned of was from a college friend, Cheryl. One Friday night, she was spending the night at her boyfriend's house, and the two of them along with her boyfriend's mom and sister— commenced a session. When, after almost an hour, nothing happened, they decided to turn in for the night. The four of them went to bed, each in different rooms, and at around three o'clock in the morning Cheryl was awakened by a feeling of unease. She sat straight up in bed and saw, standing in the doorway, a little man less than 4 feet tall, wearing a three-piece suit, with cloven hooves where his feet should have been. Before she could open her mouth, the little man threw back his head and laughed a bone-chilling and shrill laugh. A staunch Christian, Cheryl cried out, "Get out in the name of Jesus Christ!" At that point, the man took off down the hall. Cheryl shook in her bed for a long while before drifting back to sleep. In the morning, at the breakfast table, she related her frightening "dream" to the others, only to learn that the other three Ouija sitters of the night before had had the exact same experience.

It would not be long before I came nearly face to face with another bizarre Ouija-related series of events, this time at my own college, sprawling over the cornfields of Chicago's far western suburbs. I was in my third year at the time, a history major living in the upperclass, co-ed dormitory at the far end of campus. Predictably, it was just before Halloween, and typical pranks and explorations abounded as always. In fact, some friends and I had come home on the night in question after seeing *Exorcist 3* at a local theater and, afterward, exploring a nearby area famous for devil worship.

We all went to bed after a nightcap in one of our dorm rooms, preparing for a sound sleep after the decidedly non-frightening events of the evening. Sometime around 2 a.m. I awakened to the sound of sirens nearby, seemingly on our very campus. As abruptly as the sirens started, however, they simply stopped, and I fell quickly back to sleep. The next morning in the dining hall, the breakfast table was abuzz with talk of a chilling incident that had occurred during the night.

According to reports, three young men living in one of the underclass male dorms had taken a Ouija board into the monk's cemetery behind the school, where all of the priests, monks, and nuns who had worked at the school and lived at the abbey across the road were buried. Their aim was not to contact any of these souls, but to communicate with the spirit of a local woman who had been found murdered in the adjoining woods, not many years before. The stories that morning were fuzzy and muddled, but the general report was that, during the Ouija session, one of the young men had become "possessed," screeching, barking, and physically attacking his companions. Allegedly, security guards were reached, who subdued the young man and took him to his dorm room. A monk from the abbey was called who, according to the stories, sat by the boy's side as security guards held him down, praying the Rosary until paramedics arrived.

We didn't see that young man again for many days, and when he returned he was quiet and reserved, much different from the upstart he'd been before the events.

I don't know what happened that night—few likely do. Still, in the days that followed the incident, Ouija fever swept the campus, everyone attempting—with youthful curiosity and stupidity—to duplicate or even trump the whispered events. In my own dorm, some girls down the hall procured a board and were playing with it before dinner one evening. The young women later claimed nothing had happened during their session, but while they were at dinner a mysterious fire erupted in the room, though no one had been smoking and no electrical appliances were in use. In fact, a couch in the sitting room adjoining the bedroom had gone completely up in flames. The girls later told firefighters that they had left the board on the sofa when they left for dinner.

David Slone continuously collects true stories of the paranormal for his Website, *TrueGhostTales.com*, and has developed more than a passing interest in Ouija-related incidents. The following story, sent to his site from a woman named Ashley, is typical:

When I was 13 years old I had a couple of my friends sleep over on the weekend. My friends (I'll call them Brooke and Jenny) were goofing around and decided it would be a good idea to go upstairs and play with an Ouija board. They were pretty excited so I decided I would get into it as well. My mom wasn't coming home until later that night (she went to a big party).

The upstairs in my house is all one room (it was my dad's bedroom for the 14 years my mom and him were married) but my dad moved out so it was all cleared out. We set up a circle of candles, turned off the lights, and all of us sat around the Ouija board nervous and excited.

I've never played an Ouija Board before, so this was pretty nerve-[w]racking. We all placed our hands on the planchette and started asking questions like, "Is there a spirit in this room with us?" and "What's your name?" It moved to yes after a few seconds of waiting when we asked if their was a spirit in the room. At first I thought it was my friends pranking me, so I went along with it. It said it's name was Ozo or something like that. It switched its name a couple times and it never actually said a name, just these random letters.

Later me and Brooke decided to take a break, [but] Jenny stayed upstairs. We got a few drinks and some popcorn and went back upstairs to ask more questions. While our hands were on the planchette we started talking to each other about what to ask when suddenly the planchette started moving. It spelled out C-A-N-D-L-E and then went to the word "No". We asked it if it wanted us to blow out the candles, it replied with moving towards the "Yes." We were really scared to, but at the same time really anxious to see what would happen.

We all stood up except for Brooke, as she was blowing out the candles. All I remember after that was Jenny making a comment "It looks like eyes!" In the dark I could see Brooke leaning over on her knees breathing hard and not saying anything. It scared us so bad, we were screaming at the top of our lungs trying to get Brooke to say something. I was just standing there not knowing what to do when I felt something right by my shoulder whispering something in my ear. It said my name. I turned around to see who was there. I saw nothing but my friend kept saying she was seeing a pair of eyes near me. My heart was beating so fast, I kept feeling like something was behind me watching me. Brooke was still on her knees muttering about burning and pain. She started screaming and crying. At the same time something grabbed my arm and tried to pull me near the Ouija board, but I didn't let it. Jenny was just screaming at us and crying.

Eventually Jenny found the lights and turned them on. Both of us turned to Brooke to see her crying with a bloody nose. We started asking her what happened, she said the only thing she remembers was the pain and burning. I gave her Advil for her bad migraine and helped her with her bloody nose.

After that we took the Ouija board and threw it downstairs. We were still terrified and crying a little bit and went to my living room. We were just talking about what happened and the eyes Jenny kept seeing near me. She said it looked like there was some big black mist with eyes or something. We went to where we threw the Ouija board and my friend tried to pick it up, [but] it burned her. Literally, there was a burn mark on her hand like you get from a curling iron. Brooke touched it and picked it up, it didn't burn or even feel hot to her. I was too afraid to touch it so I let them deal with it. She threw it in my trash and told us to never take it out.

Later that night we watched a nice movie and drifted to sleep. In the morning my mom woke us up to ask us why we brought a Ouija board in the house. I stood up and saw it on the table (My mom is really against Ouija boards and stuff like that). She said she woke up and saw it lying in the middle of the table, we all explained to her what happened and told her we threw it in the trash. She said she never took it out and wanted me to get rid of it immediately. I took it outside and threw it in the big trash can. I kept wondering why and how it would get on the table when we remember putting it in the trash.

Through the past year we have had the Ouija board appear out of nowhere, we have tried burning it, but it wouldn't burn. We never can get rid of it.

Many opponents of the Ouija board believe that it is not just playful spirits deceiving the sitters or players, but actual demonic entities, or souls living in Hell. One of David Slone's readers relates his chilling experiences with one such soul:

I'll tell you what he told me. His name is Drew and he was a gang member from my area that died and went to hell. He said that it is very dark and smoldering hot where he is. He told me that the Ouija board is an oracle designed to talk to the residents in hell and that some spirits may be good souls that were banished to hell for not believing in God, but most of the spirits are bad spirits faking it and trying to seem good. Since my uncle knew him, he was telling me about this on multiple occasions.

From what he has told me, there are [three] stages after death. There is heaven (God's palace), limbo (our world—you are stuck here to haunt something till you move on), and hell (Satan's palace). I don't know, he said that it was too complicated to explain, but he is in hell and at the same time he is in the room with me. He said that he can be in [two] places at one time. He would warn us of demons that are coming through and said that the Ouija board is a portal to hell. They are still in hell, but half of them are in your home. That is how evil spirits are released through oracles.

He told me that hell is forever, and when he first went there he was in dark nothing with light shining on him. The light started closing and souls began to grab him and bite and suck his flesh. He screamed for mercy, but his actions were unforgivable. He said that when you go to hell, damned souls will grab you and drag you down while ripping you apart, but of course he paraphrased it. He said there is no getting out of hell. You're trapped there for good, but he said the devil allows some demons to leave so that they can damn souls.

On several sessions, Drew said he had to go because his friends were calling him and he was drinking Coronas (a beer). I found that odd: that you can drink current time beers in hell? He even talked to me while he was drunk on the board, and you could tell he was drunk because he couldn't spell. He saved my uncle one time, because my uncle is a gang member too and he told him not to go outside on a certain day. My uncle didn't believe him. My uncle sat on a plastic chair outside then I said, "Drew, if you're there give us a sign." So he grabbed the chair and pulled it out from under my uncle. We went in scared, and later that day there was a drive by and my uncle's house was shot up. He only lived because of Drew.

He said that they can read your mind, and they can either touch things or use their minds to move it. He said he can't throw anything around unless we talk to him and give him energy to do so. Also, all of them can see into the future, but they are not allowed to say much in fear of the big man. He said that if he said anything about the future, the devil would do something. And when I would ask him what, he would just repeat SAVE ME, SAVE ME, SAVE ME, SATAN, SATAN, SATAN. He was very afraid.

He would warn us and would say go to church, Satan is coming, so we were scared and ended the session. He said that the more we talk to him the more power we give him. There was once a spirit who was pretending to be Drew, and Drew came back and he told me something that amazed me. We told him what happened and he said, and I quote, "hold on—ill(sic) be back ima (sic) go kick his ass." He came back, and he said he whooped his ass. One time my dad was saying that stuff isn't real, Drew is a nobody. Drew got mad and threw the board to the ground and said leave now, he said he was going to slit my father's throat and kill him. I got on my knees and begged him to let my father be because he is ignorant. And he said RUN he is coming. We asked who was coming, and he said over and over again SATAN SATAN SATAN SATAN SATAN SATAN. So we stopped and left the board out on the porch. He would predict who would die next from a shoot out and was always correct. He also said that he raped people in hell and he was also raped in hell by a mightier spirit. He said that higher level demons will rape people in hell.

During one session, he told us to change the channel to one where it had static. He said turn on music so you can see me dance. We did, and the static was jumping up and down to the music, and that blew my mind. He said that most of the time he gets drunk in hell, but he says most of his time in hell is being tortured by demons and Satan himself. He said he looked at his face, he's looking in the face of Satan, and he told me that it is the most horrifying thing that you will ever see. He began to cry. A grown man who lived on the streets killing began to cry like a baby. Every time I ask him what does Satan look like, he starts repeating his name and says he is crying so it must be crazy scary. He also said that some people that you see on the streets are not really humans but are very powerful demons that are there to influence people to do bad things.

He did mention a demon's name that he is afraid of as well. He told me not to say his name out loud, but it was cool to write it down. He said his name is "Zetoh," and he is a pretty big baddy (sic). He also said that Succubus demons that have sex with humans are real. He told me to stop talking to him and to trust in God because he said hell is a place, a dark place and it is fiery hot. It looks like a dark fiery earth. He joked and said that they weren't kidding about the brimstones of fire and the lake of fire—it's all true. He told me to follow God so I don't ever have to see what he has seen. To answer your question on what hell is like, it looks like a battle zone on fire. He said it is worse than anyone can imagine, your brain can't even comprehend how horrific it is.

LIGHT AS A FEATHER, STIFF AS A BOARD

Generations of children—particularly girls—have played the mysterious game of "party levitation," more commonly known as "Light as a Feather." A common fixture of slumber parties, the game begins in the midst of a group of children. The elected lies on her back on the floor, while the rest of the group gathers on each side of her body, each typically placing two fingertips underneath her frame. The player with her fingers under the subject's head begins by saying:

Once, when the roads were icy and cold

The rest of the group repeats, and then the leader says:

A woman lost control of her carriage.

The group again repeats after the leader.

Finally the last part comes:

When they found her she was...

And at this point all begin to chant, *"light as a feather, stiff as a board. "*

As the chant commences, all position themselves to prepare to stand up. In many experiences, as the chant goes on, the subject indeed seems to become nearly weightless, and the children gathered are easily able to lift her by their fingertips, sometimes high above their heads. The paranormal explanation is that the spirit of the story's accident victim possesses the body of the subject, rendering her as weightless and rigid as the original, unfortunate woman.

Skeptics—indeed, most adults—believe this phenomenon is the result of self-hypnosis, in which the players subconsciously, with the aid of chanting, trick their minds into believing that the subject is weightless. Such explanations are backed up by the well-known stories of car accidents, in which loved ones are rescued by family members or friends who suddenly and somehow have the strength to rip off the car door or lift or push it off the victim. Alternately, many believe this is a simple case of weight distribution, wherein a heavy object is easily lifted if the weight of it is evenly distributed, even among a group of six or eight prepubescent girls.

In the summer of 1665, the great diarist Samuel Pepys recorded an incideny of "Light as a Feather" that had been reported to him by a colleague. The colleague, who hailed from Bordeaux, France, related to Pepys how he had once witnessed

> ...four little girles, very young ones, all kneeling, each of them, upon one knee; and one begun the first line, whispering in the eare of the next, and the second to the third, and the third to the fourth, and she to the first. Then the first begun the second line, and so round quite through, and putting each one finger only to a boy that lay flat upon his back on the ground, as if he was dead; at the end of the words, they did with their four fingers raise this boy high as they could reach....

Amazed, Pepys's friend wondered if the young boy was indulging in some sort of trickery, or if he was perhaps just very light. So he decided to bring out one of his servants to test the childrens' true abilities. He called "the cook of the house, a very lusty fellow...who is very big, and they did raise him in just the same manner."

BLOODY MARY AND OTHER URBAN LEGENDS

An enduringly popular supernatural ritual among young people is that of "Bloody Mary," also known as Mary Worth, Mary Worthington, Hell Mary, Kathy, Sally, or Black Aggie, to name a few variations. The ritual requires the subject to go into a darkened room, preferably a bathroom with no windows, and turn off the lights. Gazing into the mirror, the subject then calls on the spirit with a specified invocation, for example, a standard chant of "Bloody Mary, Bloody Mary," "I believe in Mary Worth" or "Kathy, Come Out!" In some local versions, the subject is required to spin around three times or run the water in the sink or bathtub. In Brazil, the bathroom spirit is known as "a loira do banheiro" or "the blonde in the toilet," and is called out by flushing the toilet. According to the story, when the spirit or witch spirit comes forth, she will scratch your face, tear out your eyes, rip off your arms, or perform some other brutal act, leaving the victim maimed and bloody. By some accounts, she will drag the subject back into the mirror with her, never to be seen again.

S.E. Schlosser, in her book, *Spooky Pennsylvania*, retells an old story based in Harrisburg, in which a woman named Mary, reported to be a witch, was said to have lured a number of young women of the town to her forest home. There, she would drain them of their blood, drinking it to regain youth and beauty, and then bury the bodies in shallow woodland graves. According to legend, the townspeople captured and burned "Bloody Mary," but while she burned, Mary called a curse upon her killers. She claimed that anyone who dared to say her name into a mirror would call out her vengeful spirit, and that she would tear them each to shreds, as she had been torn apart by the knives and pitchforks of her attackers.

Chicago became internationally famous for a Bloody Mary–style legend with the release of the film, *Candyman*, in the 1990s. The film, based on a short story by horror novelist Clive Barker, told the tale of a young black man—a former slave and gifted painter—who came north to Chicago to pursue a career as a portrait artist. When he was commissioned to paint the portrait of a former abolitionist's daughter, painter and subject fell in love. However, when the father learned of their union, his true colors shone through. He hired a group of ruffians to find the young artist and destroy him. The attackers accosted him, dragged him to a field near an apiary, and cut off his right arm, which he used for painting. Then, they covered his body with honey from the apiary's beehives and released several hives of bees, who stung young man to death. In the film, a young graduate student is researching urban legends and discovers that a string of brutal murders at a notorious Chicago housing project are being blamed on the spirit of the murdered artist—known in death as "Candyman" because of the sweetness of the honey that covered him at death. Candyman is a vindictive spirit who comes forth for vengeance when unbelievers call his name. The ritual requires the subject to go into a darkened bathroom, Bloody Mary–style—and call out the name of Candyman five times. What happens to the unbelieving graduate student in the film is that, well, she becomes a believer when she dares to play the "game."

Boarded up buildings of Cabrini-Green, now mostly demolished, were party of Chicago's most notorious housing project. The development was believed my many of the city's children to have been the home of the notorious "Candyman." *(Photograph by Peter Van den Bossche.)*

Clive Barker created the story of *Candyman*; it is not based on any real piece of Chicago history. However, in addition to the inspiration from Bloody Mary folklore, some believe that Barker was also influenced by a sort of "real life" urban legend figure in his home town of Liverpool, England. In the 1980s, Liverpool youths were shaken to a frenzy by a character known as "Purple Aki," believed by many to be an urban legend. Purple Aki was, according to reports, a towering, black bodybuilder who stalked young men, often sodomizing them and carving his initials in their buttocks with an army knife. Boys and young men lived in fear of this elusive predator, many of whom dropped out of sports teams and gyms because of fear of "the Purple One," and in Liverpool, men (not boys) worked pre-dawn paper routes. Adults who grew up during the reign of Purple Aki remember what a shocking impact the legend had on their childhoods, keeping them from playgrounds, woods, back-yard camping, and even evening walks through their neighborhoods. Stories abounded that he had been killed many times, or that he had drowned in a nearby woodland pool, but was later seen quite alive. No one had ever caught him and no adults seemed to see him. He was believed my many to not exist at all.

Amazingly, in 2003, after a 20-year reign of terror over the young men of Liverpool, a local man named Akinwale Arobieke was arrested and jailed after trying to touch a young man's biceps. Almost immediately, he was recognized by dozens of young men—some by now middle-aged—to be the legendary "Purple Aki" who had terrorized their younger years.

My research into ghost stories of Chicago led me, one summer, to visit many branches of the Chicago Public Library system, where I would speak with children about their experiences with the paranormal. Time and again I found that the story of Candyman is believed to be a real one, and that many Chicago children do believe that the crime and death that surrounds them and fills their lives comes from his diabolical hand, and that if you don't believe it you can bring him out with the tried and true mirror ritual.

When I was a child growing up in Chicago, before Candyman came to town, our local version of the legend required us to invoke "Mary Worth." When I grew up and began researching local ghost stories, I met a man named Larry Rawn who shared a story with me that may have been the historical basis of our own Chicago "Bloody Mary" ritual. Rawn lives in Gurnee, Illinois, about an hour north of the city. Today, Gurnee is a sprawling suburb, known for shopping malls, indoor water parks, and Six Flags, but it was once a quaint and quiet old town along the Lake Michigan shoreline.

According to the legend, in the days of the Civil War, a woman named Mary Worth lived on a Gurnee farm. She, too, was believed to be a witch. It was discovered that Mary was capturing slaves who had come north to freedom, and that she had shackled the men in her barn, forcing them to care for her animals, and in her home, forcing the women to cook, clean, sew, and tend to her needs. When the townspeople found out about Mary's slaves—who verified that she had also been practicing witchcraft—they descended upon the farm, released her captives, shackled her inside the house, and burned the property to the ground with Mary inside. Mary was allegedly buried outside the walls of the local cemetery, and while the "game" of "Mary Worth" may be played in any bathroom, many young people make evening journeys to the graveyard itself to call upon the spirit of Mary Worth. Assembling after midnight, the brave stand around her grave and chant, "I believe in Mary Worth," hoping the witch's spirit will reward their courage. Curiously, I have seen, over the years, a number of photographs taken at the site of young women with their faces scratched and bleeding. These young women all claim that no one touched them— that the scratches appeared from out of nowhere.

Role Playing With Fire?

The controversy over role playing games began with the games' beginnings. Critics of role-playing games quickly came to believe that the games—especially the ground-breaking *Dungeons & Dragons*—bred antisocial behavior, depression, and violence. Not long after, opponents such as the very vocal Bill Schnoebelen—a former witch and vampire—called the game "essentially a feeding program for occultism and witchcraft." In this New Age, such charges may not be all that upsetting to a lot of non-Christians, or to Christians who think of occultism and witchcraft as related to Judeo-Christian practices. Much of the philosophy of Schnoebelen and others does stem from Christianity; Christians are told by Scripture to "abstain from all appearance of evil." It's clear that, as Schnoebelen observes, "much of the trappings, art, figurines, and writing within D&D certainly appear evil—to say the least of it."

Beyond the Christian right, even practicing pagans, witches, and occultists agree that putting magical recipes into unschooled hands is never, ever a good idea. Schnoebelen points out a somewhat practical issue with the seemingly harmless game of Dungeons & Dragons, claiming that

> [T]he materials themselves, in many cases, contain authentic magical rituals. I can tell you this from my own experience. I was a witch high priest (Alexandrian tradition) during the period 1973–84. During some of that period (1976–80) I was also involved in hardcore Satanism. We studied and practiced and trained more than 175 people in the Craft. Our "covendom" was in Milwaukee, Wisconsin:

just a short drive away from the world headquarters of TSR, the company which makes Dungeons & Dragons, in Lake Geneva, WI. In the late 1970s, a couple of the game writers actually came to my wife and I as prominent "sorcerers" in the community. They wanted to make certain the rituals were authentic. For the most part, they are.

These two guys sat in our living room and took copious notes from us on how to make sure the rituals were truly right "from the book" (this meaning that they actually came from magic grimoires or workbooks). They seemed satisfied with what they got and left us thankfully.

Again, Christian culture has been concerned about the spiritual implications of D&D since the game's release, and even non-Christians have gotten involved in the fight against its manufacture. Schnoebelen reports that

[B]ack in 1986, a fellow appeared on "The 700 Club" (a Christian television program) who was a former employee and game writer for TSR. He testified right on the show that he got into a wrangle with the management there because he saw that the rituals were too authentic and could be dangerous. He protested to his boss and was basically told that this was the intent—to make the games as real as possible. He felt conscience-stricken (even though he was not a Christian at the time), and felt he had to resign from the company.

Now, the question becomes—if a person "innocently" works an authentic ritual that conjures up a demon, or curses someone; thinking that they are only playing a game—might not the ritual still have efficacy? I think we know the answer to that question. If you play at shooting your friend in the head with what you think is an unloaded pistol and don't know a shell is in the chamber, is your friend any less dead because you were playing?

...To quote an old proverb: "Though the boys throw stones at the frogs in sport, the frogs die in earnest."

Many may scoff at the pleas of self-identified Christians, thinking them overly concerned with the game of D&D—and erroneously blameful of demons when its players take a bad turn. Surely, those who go over the edge with D&D in their lives have more secular problems—or do they?

Bill Schnoebelen compiled a D&D "Hall of Shame," including deaths, suicides, and ritual acts of torture or abuse by D&D players. Some supporters of the game have come forward to protest that other factors in these cases were much more influential than the game. Whether you believe or not that diabolical creatures played a part, there's no question that demons—whether spirits or the demons of mental illness—were there, every time:

Bill Schnoebelen's D&D "Hall of Shame"

1. The "Freeway Killer," Vernon Butts, who committed suicide in his cell in 1987 while being

held as a suspect in a string of murders, was an avid D&D player.

2. D&D player (14 years old) commits suicide by hanging, 1979. Name withheld by parents' request.

3. D&D player (17 years old) Michael Dempsey, Lynnwood, Washington. Suicide by gunshot wound to the head, May 1981. Witnesses saw him trying to summon up D&D demons just minutes before his death.

4. D&D player (? years old) Steve Loyacano, Castle Rock, Colorado. Suicide by carbon monoxide poisoning, October 1982. Police report that Satanic writings in a suicide note linked the death to D&D.

5. D&D player (21 years old) Timothy Grice, Lafayette, Colorado. Suicide by shotgun blast, January 1983. Detective reports noted, "D&D became a reality. He thought he was not constrained to this life, but could leave [it] and return because of the game."

6. D&D player (18 years old) Harold T. Collins, Marion, Ohio. Suicide by hanging, April 1983. Collins was noted to be "possessed" by D&D as if he were living the game.

7. D&D player (16 years old) Daniel Erwin, Lafayette, Colorado. Murder by brother's shotgun blast to head, November 1984. Death was apparently the result of a death pact as part of the game.

8. D&D player (12 years old) Steve Erwin (see above) suicide by gunshot, November 1984. Detective report stated: "No doubt D&D cost them their lives."

9. D&D player (no age given) Joseph Malin, Salt Lake City, Utah. Pled guilty to first degree murder, March 1988, and was sentenced to life in prison. He killed a 13-year-old girl while acting out the fantasy-role game. The girl had been raped, her throat cut, and she had been stabbed twice in the chest. Police said his "violent urges were fed by extreme involvement in the fantasy role-playing game Dungeons and Dragons.'"

10. D&D player (14 years old) Sean Sellers was convicted of killing his parents and a convenience store clerk in Greeley, Oklahoma, January 1987. He is the youngest inmate of death row in the country as of this writing (22 now). His involvement in hard-core Satanism began with D&D, according to his own testimony.

11. D&D player (14 years old) Tom Sullivan, Jr., of Amarillo, Texas, became involved in Satanism and ended up stabbing his mother to death in January 1988, arranging a ritual circle (from D&D) in the middle of the living room floor and lighting a fire in its midst. Fortunately, his dad and little brother were awakened by a smoke detector. By then, however, Tom, Jr. had slashed his wrists and throat with his Boy Scout knife and died in the snow in a neighbor's yard.

As children emerge from childhood and enter into adolescence, their unconscious minds, struggling to define (and reject or accept), takes many forms. Forced either deliberately or unconsciously to discard their paranormal beliefs and abilities, young people are forced to seek the paranormal in places where the phenomena and its beliefs are seen as "all in fun." Games like "Light as a Feather, Stiff as a Board" or "Bloody Mary" keep the thrilling door to the paranormal open, while convincing parents that paranormal belief has been relegated to its proper place in their children's lives. But although some games may be harmless, is there another, very real dimension to these pastimes? The power of the Ouija board or of role-playing games have puzzled and concerned a generation of parents, some of whom have watched their children's social and emotional lives disintegrate through involvement in these "harmless" pursuits. But are the "demons" unleashed by these simple toys really supernatural in origin? Or, rather, are these unfortunate young people being drawn into the darkest corners of their own unconscious minds?

10

AUTISM'S INSIGHTS

Many are aware that adolescents usually serve as the agents in poltergeist cases, unwittingly upsetting the force fields of random or significant objects with their own displaced energies. What most don't know is that, in the world of parapsychological research, children are proving responsible for much more than the chaotic activity of the poltergeist. In fact, many autistic children in particular seem to demonstrate significant psi abilities—abilities that- they seem able to control much more easily than "normal" children or adults. Many people are discovering what the families and friends of autistic children have known for a long time: These deeply misunderstood children may exist on a higher spiritual plane; they exhibit a deep empathy with both people and with animals, and are often able to "teach" these abilities to those around them.

Judith Lecuyer, mother of an autistic boy named Ben, was used to living in a slightly different household. Little Ben had habits that were difficult to live with, some of them symptoms of the mysterious condition called autism. Lecuyer was used to carrying Ben up the three flights of stairs to their apartment (he refused to use stairs but would climb up on to the furniture with delight), but she didn't quite know what to think when dangerous objects began to appear in Ben's hiding places. These were objects that had been deliberately placed in high, locked cabinets, well out of reach of a 2 year old, yet they appeared again and again. Similar events con- tinued to cause Lecuyer to wonder if something paranormal was going on. While the children were strapped into their feeding chairs in the dining room, a Winnie-the-Pooh cake on the sideboard found its way into the baby's lap. When questioned about the cake, Lecuyer's older son said that, while buckled into his chair 7 feet away, Ben had made the cake fly. The moment of truth came one day in the family's kitchen, when an empty two-liter soda bottle became the object of Ben's desire. Unable to reach it, Ben stared intently at the bottle. Lecuyer tells how his little face became beet red, and she watched as the bottle "shimmied and trembled and gently bounced its way to the edge."

After years of talking with the parents of other autistic children, Lucuyer discovered that telekinesis is so common among autistic children that she wondered if such abilities would someday be included among the criteria for diagnosis! Some signs of telekinesis may be, for example, objects stored out of the child's reach that appear in the child's special hiding places; items falling or shooting off shelves; and glass objects breaking or shattering without being touched. Sometimes, the telekinesis is obvious. Lucuyer's son often accomplished the movement of objects (like the soda bottle) by staring intently at them, his face becoming hot and flushed, until they moved, fell over, or rolled toward him. He also enjoyed making objects spin under his gaze, such as wind chimes, hanging plants, and so on. Ben's telekinetic abilities were so recurrent—so "normal"—that his mother had to establish limits on his exercise of them, as any parent would limit other potentially disruptive or destructive activities. She also points out that, usually, there are emotions behind these semi-mischievous activities that need to be recognized: boredom, or sometimes impatience or anger.

Frequently, family members like Lecuyer report that, at an early age in the autistic child's life, the parents and siblings became aware of receiving images and messages from the child via paranormal means: a type of communication called telepathy. With Ben, it was at the most frustrating moments—when communication seemed hopeless—that he would press his forehead against the forehead of his mother, father, brother, or sister. And what followed was always a moment of clarity: instant knowledge—without a word—of what Ben needed, wanted, or felt.

Non-autistic children, adults, and their families aren't typically able to use their telepathic abilities at will. If I press my forehead against yours, it's unlikely that I will suddenly know you are hungry or thirsty, or want to dance. Parapsychologists are starting to think it's because we don't have to. Often, even those with motor or vocal impairments have alternate means of normal communication. If one cannot physically write or type, one can still speak—to another person or a machine that will transform that speech into writing. If one cannot speak, writing and typing are always there. Likely, it is the lack of any channel of "normal" communication—speech or writing—that forces autistic families to a place where they're desperate to communicate, and it's that desperation that starts the psi powers flowing.

Lecuyer offers some additional clues as to whether your young child—autistic or not—is trying to communicate with you without the benefit of language. Aside from the forehead-to-forehead pressing, does your child grasp your fingers or thumb emphatically, and for long periods of time, make prolonged eye contact, or place your hand right over his or her heart, wanting you to keep it there quietly? If any of these do occur, are these actions accompanied by images that appear in your mind, or even intuitive or "gut feelings" about what your child is feeling or thinking?

Sometimes telepathy in families with autism crosses over into the realm of "remote viewing," another controversial paranormal ability. Remote viewing made headlines in the 1990s, after the declassification of documents revealed details of the so-called Stargate Project, a multimillion-dollar research program funded by the U.S. government. Stargate aimed to determine whether remote viewing—the ability to identify objects at a distance via paranormal perception— and other ostensibly paranormal abilities might have any military use. Though Stargate was terminated in 1995 due to its failure to demonstrate a value for intelligence-gathering, remote viewing is still believed by quite a few researchers to, in fact, exist, albeit with less-than-world-changing applications. Lecuyer writes of an incident in which Ben's father was shopping and felt "an overwhelming urge" to purchase for Ben a shirt depicting the cartoon characters from the television program, *Blue's Clues.* When Dad returned home, Ben lunged for the bag, delighted. Mom then reported that, the entire time Dad was gone, Ben had been sitting on his bed, staring hypnotically at a stuffed *Blue's Clues* doll. Lucuyer wonders if that experience went beyond the family's "ordinary" telepathy and crossed over into the area of remote viewing, so that Ben actually saw his father, and the shirt, in the store, and only then used his telepathic abilities to influence his father's actions.

Many parents and caregivers believe that autistic children use telepathy to engage in one of their most intriguing activities: communicating with animals. Whereas many children seem to exhibit the ability to converse with animals on some level, this ability can be stunning in autistics. Author William Stillman, himself an adult with Asperger's Syndrome (a highly functioning form of autism), has authored a number of books about the very special place of autistics in society today. In *Autism and the God Connection,* Stillman relates the story of Patrick, a young autistic boy living on a farm in Pennsylvania. At the age of 14, Patrick's family purchased a horse who had been severely abused by her former owners. For the rest of the family, getting the horse to trust them was a long, difficult process, and one that never ended; though her trust of them improved, the horse would always be nervous, easily agitated, and fearful. However, from the beginning, the autistic boy was able to wave his hands in front of the horse, pull at her mane, and touch her in places the horse would not normally tolerate. The horse endured all of these actions with stoic calm, but only from the autistic child. As for the mechanism of communication, Patrick himself told his caregiver, using a letter board to spell, that he and the horse would send and receive mental pictures between each other's minds.

This same boy's mother also tells of Patrick's natural appeal to cats and dogs, despite the fact that, as an autistic, he would not "befriend" them or show them affection and, in fact, demonstrated fear in front of them. Lack of affection typically keeps dogs from coming near or bonding with people, and showing fear drives both cats and dogs away, but in all cases, cats and dogs would come up to Patrick over and over, before coming to any of the others present, no matter how affectionate the others would be.

Another parent related to Stillman an account of her own autistic son who was attractive to butterflies. Time and again, she would find him reading or just sitting outside, with a butterfly sitting on his shoulder, or butterflies flutteringly quietly around him while he played.

Possibly the greatest apparent breakthrough in autism research has become, for many, its most disappointing and heartbreaking. When Ben Lecuyer was very young, older autistics were becoming part of a revolutionary movement centered on the use of keyboards or "letter boards," which were ostensibly allowing those on the autistic spectrum to communicate through typing or pointing to letters of the alphabet, with the aid of a "facilitator" who would gently hold the autistic's hand or elbow during the communications. The theory behind "facilitated communication" (FC) is that the facilitator provides a steadying or centering influence on the autistic, which allows the student to focus his energy—both mental and physical—and write.

Suddenly, many autistic children and adults, the sweeping majority of whom were previously classified as mentally retarded, were communicating thoughts and feelings at the level of their peers. In fact, in many cases the spelling and grammar of the communications were perfect, and oftentimes stunningly lucid and insightful thoughts came through. The FC movement was part of a growing trend among the researchers and caregivers of autistics: Once seen as a curse upon the autistic and his family, the "affliction" of autism started to be seen as something quite different, and some began to wonder if autistics hold the key to a much deeper understanding of a much wider world.

Heartbreakingly, as FC enthusiasm spread around the world, problems followed, their circumstances sometimes as shocking as FC itself. Skepticism about the method had begun early on, and around the world puzzled researchers sought to determine how autistic children could somehow learn to read and write perfectly without the benefit of normal instruction, and whether their often-moving communications were actually theirs or those of their facilitators, somehow consciously or unconsciously influencing their movements.

Supporters of FC believe that because many autistic children are today schooled in normal classrooms, the prevalence of letters, numbers, and words in the environment are enough to teach spelling and grammar, and that autistics actually comprehend and engage in the teaching around them, despite the fact that their bodies, their faces, and their emotions seem detached and distracted. Their absolutely capable minds, as it were, are basically trapped in uncooperative bodies. Those suspicious of the method, however, were unconvinced, and a number of experiments ensued, seeking to find whether autistics and their facilitators could actually pass FC through the lens of hard science.

One of the most common and often duplicated FC experiments was a simple one: show the autistic subject a photograph of an object—a boat, a tree, a shoe—and show the facilitator another, each different, each from the other. Then ask the autistic to write the word with the aid of the facilitator. Such experiments gained worldwide recognition through a special report done by Frontline, which aired in 1993, in which researchers revealed overwhelming rates of failure. In fact, one experimenter's trials produced not a single accurate answer from their autistic subjects. Instead, time after time, the autistic subjects wrote the words describing their facilitator's photos.

The laboratory experiments were disappointing in the extreme. In many cases, facilitators had found their lives' callings in the remarkable breakthrough of FC. But their heartbreak and discouragement were far from the worst of it.

Across the nation, researchers were becoming aware of a disturbing trend among FC participants. Accusations of sexual abuse, accusing one or another parent—and in one case both parents and a grandparent living with the family— began to turn up with shocking frequency. In each case, the allegations proved to be unfounded, though they had often resulted in one or more parents being driven from the home or, devastatingly, the autistic child being placed in foster care.

To this day, experts are uncertain about the impetus for these widespread allegations. Though experts say it's clear that they were coming from the unconscious minds of the facilitators themselves, why were false accusations materializing at all? Did the facilitators somehow unconsciously suspect abuse at the homes of their autistics? Were the facilitators abused themselves, and these allegations repressed memories surfacing during FC sessions? Or was something else going on?

The expert conclusion drawn on the entire situation and presented to the *Frontline* audience, interestingly, referenced a paranormal communication tool, the talking or Ouija board, in explaining the mechanism at play:

> Far from unlocking the minds of autistic individuals FC tapped the unconscious thoughts of the facilitator. The process, experts say, is not unlike what goes on with a Ouija board. As letters are built up, hypotheses form about what comes next. The facilitator...is unaware that they are controlling the typing.

Thus, a few words are typed, the unconscious picks up a thread somewhere, and the FC starts to flow. In light of this theory, it is perhaps not surprising that, among the many thousands of individuals engaged in FC, perhaps a few dozen should have "revealed" tales of abuse.

What's less easy to understand is the physical mechanism of FC, especially when students advance to the point where they no longer are being physically aided by the facilitator. While watching video of facilitators literally holding the arms, hands, or even fingers of their autistic companions as they type or point to their letter boards, it's simple to believe that the facilitators are able to physically manipulate the communications, either consciously or unconsciously, but what about when there is no touching at all?

To deliberately take this into the realm of the paranormal, might it be possible that autistics are so in tune with their facilitators that they are subconsciously channeling the facilitators' very thoughts, without the need for physical manipulation? Some autistics say they feel for the heartbeat of their facilitator, and so the hand of the facilitator on their shoulder—and the sensing of the faint pulse in his hand is enough to begin the FC. This would support proponents' theories that the facilitator is a steadying or centering influence on the autistic, but maybe there is more than just stability that is being "taken" from the facilitator. Maybe emotions, thoughts, memories—and the words that describe them—are being unconsciously channeled as well.

Have they become skilled in centering or focusing their bodies and thoughts, have they become so intuned to their facilitators that they are channeling the helper's thoughts without even touching, or are they—as skeptics still maintain—being aided by facilitators who frequently though perhaps unconsciously "adjust" their keyboards or letter boards and call it "independent?" One scene on the Frontline special shows a patient with cerebral palsy using a pointer to make his own decision on where to live, whether in a nursing home or with his parents. A line drawn on the screen where the video is shown makes it clear that the facilitator is moving the paper where the choices are written, either consciously or unconsciously, directing the unmoving pointer to the choice of "nursing home."

Professional skeptics, understandably, continue to have a field day with the FC movement. Once again, it's interesting that problems with parapsychology are used to justify some of their criticisms. A writer for the Internet resource *The Skeptic's Dictionary* bemusedly discusses one of the conditions supposedly necessary for FC:

> [B]elievers in FC claim that it only works when a special bond has been established between facilitator and patient. It is interesting that the parents and other loved ones who have been bonding with the patient for years are unable to be facilitators with their own children. FC needs a kind stranger to work. And when the kind strangers and their patients are put to the test, they generally fail. We are told that is because the conditions made them nervous. These ad hoc excuses sound familiar; they sound like the complaints of parapsychologists.

Despite such disgusted summations, however, FC—and the even more extraordinary claims of telepathy, telekinesis, clairvoyance of ghosts, communication with animals, and remote viewing—continue to convince parents, caregivers, and many researchers that the special connections between the autistic and the unknown are part of autistics' very different, and much more sensitive and finely tuned world.

Writing about *Autism and the God Connection,* Stillman reminds us of Freud's belief that telepathy is

> a primitive form of communication made dormant by language. If...we were all suddenly rendered mute indefinitely, without any means to communicate, we would eventually gravitate into little colonies where we'd instinctively intuit one another's thoughts and feelings without words.

Speaking of the spiritual experiences of autistics, his special concern, Stillman believes that "(c)hildren and animals, as the purest of innocents, often perceive spiritual experiences only because they haven't yet been conditioned *not to.*" Autistic children, then, with their naturally high sensitivity, just may be living on an essentially different plane. And it may be one that non-autistics may never reach, at least in this lifetime.

11

THE CHILDREN OF NOW

INDIGO-COLORED GLASSES?

The Indigo Children were the first generation of "special" children who are believed to have ushered in a new stage of human evolution, with the first births of these children beginning in the 1970s. Indigo children were first named by Nancy Ann

Tappe, a psychic who outlined the concept in her 1982 book, *Understanding Your Life Through Color.* Tappe claimed that, beginning in the 1960s, she found that many more children were being born with indigo-colored auras, and that these children possessed common traits such as intense empathy, deep spirituality, curiosity, and independence. Tappe's conceptualization of "Indigo children" was greatly popularized by a later book, *The Indigo Children*, by Lee Carroll and Jan Tober, whose authors suggested that these children were sent into the world with a unified purpose: to banish wars, clean up the environment, and restore healthy eating habits.

Critics of the Indigo movement believe that children classified as "Indigo" are actually suffering from attention-deficit hyperactivity disorder (ADHD), and that labeling one's child as "Indigo" is a way to avoid facing the reality of illness—and the medications that would accompany medical diagnosis. Interestingly, supporters of the Indigo movement claim that Indigo children do not function well in "normal" environments because they don't recognize conventional authorities, that educators are not capable of understanding their superior intellect, and that the children do not have feelings of guilt and, thus, cannot be disciplined. Practically, this means that many of the "special" traits of so-called Indigos are overwhelmingly disruptive to their less-progressive peers. Entitlement, arrogance, superiority, and refusal to follow rules: These are just a few of the exceptional qualities of Indigos that have driven many Indigo parents to homeschool their children and give up on discipline and rules altogether.

Not surprisingly, the categorization of Indigos has enraged a whole generation of their peers, who see their "special traits" as evidence of nothing more than bad parenting and self-indulgence. According to one critic, "Perhaps these Indigo Children are actually a menace to humanity, and should be blown up as in *Village of the Damned.*"

PROGRESSION

The second generation of special children is that of the "Crystal children." According to expert Celia Fenn, these children began coming to earth around the year 2000, and are preparing the Earth for the opening of the Ninth Dimension of Consciousness—the consciousness of Christ—which will be opened around 2012.

Crystal children are, in some ways, easier to recognize than their Indigo brothers and sisters. They are usually huge babies with large heads, and they tend to have big eyes that they use for staring a lot. Experts claim that this is their way of "reading" a person's soul, and in fact these children are purported to have telepathic abilities: to paranormally know things about others. Unlike Indigos—who often come across as narcissistic or even sociopathic—Crystals are intensely sensitive and nurturing, and are said to be deeply aware of the tension and resentments of others, especially family members. Crystals are believed to exhibit fearlessness, often to their physical detriment. They are clumsy in their physical bodies and do not seem to understand the functioning or limitations of the physical form.

Prone to tantrums, demands, outbursts, and other problematic behaviors, Crystals are excused as highly creative:

We are warned to allow them to create their own realities without our structures and limitations.

Many children who do not begin to speak at a normal age have been labeled as Crystals, generally by anguished parents who gladly accept the New Age theory that their children have been communicating through "higher" methods such as soul reading and telepathy. Some parents claim that their Crystals are able to read entire books without opening them.

A much-discussed trait of so-called Crystals is the ability to heal themselves, other humans, and animals. Some parents claim to have observed such healings before their Crystal child's first birthday.

The Next Generation

According to experts such as New Age guru Doreen Virtue, the next and youngest wave of special children is that of the so-called Rainbow children, the third generation. Born at the turn of the Millenium and after, the Rainbows are being born from the previous generation of Crystals. According to those who claim to understand them, Rainbows come into life with no past lives—and thus no karma to make up for. Whereas other generations may have incarnated into dysfunctional families in order to grow spiritually, Rainbows do not "choose" unstable families to live in, but happy, settled, nurturing ones. Rainbows are reportedly both totally fearless and trusting, and must be guarded against both being taken advantage of, abused, or abducted, as well as against putting themselves in physical peril.

Virtue says that Rainbows are healers, and are born with the healing energies of Reiki and QiGong, which had to be learned by previous generations. Those who have been born already were the "scouts" or forerunners of the population boom, which has just begun and will last, it is said, until 2030.

Virtue writes that the Rainbows are

...perfectly balanced in their male and female energies. They are confident without aggressiveness; they are intuitive and psychic without effort; they are magical and can bend time, become invisible, and go without sleep and food.

...The purpose of the Rainbow children is to complete the final stages of the foundation that the Indigo and Crystal children have made. The three children, Indigo, Crystal, and Rainbow each have a specific task. The Indigo children are to break down the paradigm of the traditional thinking. Then the Crystal children will build their foundation on the broken paradigm. Finally, the Rainbow children are here to build on to what the Indigo and Crystal children began.

One wonders at the reality underlying the incredibly New Agey theories regarding the Children of Now: three generations of children born at the end of the first modern century—a century of world wars; the collapse of traditional values; the breaking of a million paradigms and rules, hopes, and limitations; the deepening of sensitivities between races, classes, and lifestyles. Have these children really been sent—or sent themselves—to save the human race? Or are they the natural result of social, intellectual, and emotional evolution?

EPILOGUE

*Alice laughed. "There's no use trying," she said;
"one can't believe impossible things."
"I daresay you haven't had much practice," said the
Queen. "When I was younger, I always did it for half
an hour a day. Why, sometimes I've believed as many
as six impossible things before breakfast."*

—from Alice Through the Looking Glass

...Say them with me, Alice:
One, there is a drink that makes you shrink.
Two, there are cakes that make you grow.
Three, cats can disappear.
Four, animals can talk.
Five, there is a place called Wonderland.
Six, I can slay the Jabberwocky."

—*from the film,* Alice in Wonderland *(2010)*

The world of children is vastly different from our adult world. What does a child's world really look like? In fact, it's a fairytale kind of place where seemingly anything can happen. There are fairies, gnomes, and goblins. Time travel is possible, animals talk, and toys come to life. Remarkably, there are truly monsters in the closet and under the bed. So what can we do to help our children understand these experiences, accept the good ones, and protect themselves from the bad ones?

COMMUNICATE

1. Listen to your children. Listen to what they're saying about what's happening to them. Listen to what they're afraid of.

2. Believe there may be something going on.

3. Ask your children about their experiences. Even if they don't seem to see ghosts, have invisible friends, talk to the dog, or remember past lives, make it clear that you accept these experiences as

part of life. Talk about your own experiences, but be careful not to instill more fear.

4. To help prevent serious problems, such as poltergeist occurrences and possessions, encourage your children early on to express their feelings and opinions

Take Simple Measures Against Negative Entities

1. Practice your religion and make it part of your home. Teach your children that good—whether it's a force or a god—is more powerful than negativity. Make sure your home and you children's rooms have reminders of this faith.

2. Even if you're not sure you believe in them, help your children battle the "Negs," or negative entities, by simply keeping on a night light, keeping music on low, etc. Open the closet door at night and put a light inside. Fear of the closet is such a disturbing and all-encompassing thing. There's no need for it. Author Robert Bruce might also suggest that you watch their sleep patterns and make sure they are getting the proper sleep. If your children seem disturbed, it may help to carry your children across running water—even a garden hose—or put them in the shower. You know how relaxed you feel after swimming or taking a bath? Many people believe this is because the water breaks the hold of negative entities.

ENCOURAGE SAFE EXPLORATION OF THE PARANORMAL

1. When children are very young, start with kindness to nature. Get a book that teaches them how to make a fairy garden. Encourage your children to sit quietly with your pets and to try to understand their feelings. Teach about the seasons, about the phases of the moon, and talk about the mysterious ways in which these things affect us.

2. Dispel the fear of dying and death by making trips to cemeteries, learning about their history, and about those buried there. Go to haunted places, if your children want to. In Chicago, there is an alley behind the Oriental Theater in the Loop, and it's called Death's Alley. My children love going there, which at times mortifies me, because of what happened there—the death of many schoolchildren in a terrible fire 100 years ago. But children identify with this story because of the children, and they are drawn to history and compassion because of it.

3. Teach the science of ghost hunting. Encourage your children to take photographs and to use simple tools, like a compass, to study ghosts. Discourage reckless attempts at spirit communication, such as the Ouija board, and focus on things that have proven to be safer: like EVP and dowsing rods, and emphasize simply learning about what's there rather than trying to "conjure up" things that aren't.

When It Gets Scary

1. If ghosts in your house are scaring your children, get rid of them! This is easier to do than you might think. Have your children tell it to go away because it's scary, and your children can even sweep it out the door. I've been investigating ghosts for more than 20 years, and this works 90 percent of the time. If the method does fail, use prayers from your religious background to quell the troubles.

2. If your children are having real problems that seem to be paranormal in nature, get help, but be careful who you ask. You don't want to end up with someone who just wants your money. This is a very tricky business because there are so many people and organizations on the Internet today, all wanting to help those with ghostly problems. Many people have had good luck writing to scientific foundations like the Rhine Research Center or the Society for Psychical Research. These organizations run on very little money, but their members are devoted to understanding paranormal phenomena and are educated and experienced. Many researchers today specialize in children's abilities and experiences, especially with past lives, psychokinesis, and autism-related abilities.

Above all else, keep the first point close to your heart and *listen*. This cannot be stressed enough. Remember that our children are living in a different world than we are, and it's terrifying for them to be there alone. Let them know that you understand that your world is different, and let them know that you want to know about theirs, and to help them be happy and safe in it.

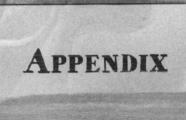

APPENDIX

RESOURCES FOR FURTHER INFORMATION AND ASSISTANCE

Society for Psychical Research: Founded in 1882 by leading British intellectuals, the SPR was dedicated to investigating those kinds of phenomena that suggest that we humans are something more than mere biological machines, phenomena such as telepathy, clairvoyance, precognition, psychokinesis, and postmortem survival. Publishes essential reading in parapsychology, the *Journal of the Society for Psychical Research.*

Website: *www.spr.ac.uk*

Rhine Research Center: Long the major research center in the United States, continuing the work started by J. B. and Louisa Rhine at Duke University in the 1930s. Publishes the *Journal of Parapsychology,* one of the essential scientific journals for keeping up with the latest developments in parapsychology.

Website: *www.rhine.org*

Parapsychological Association (PA): The scientific and scholarly organization in the field. Election to full membership in the PA comes with demonstrated scientific and scholarly contributions to the field. Student or associate membership is available also.

Website: *www.parapsych.org*

Parapsychology Foundation (PF): The publisher of the *International Journal of Parapsychology,* one of the essential scientific journals to read to keep up with the latest parapsychology developments. The PF also provides small grants for scientific parapsychology and has one of the best libraries around.

Website: *www.parapsychology.org*

American Society for Psychical Research: The oldest organization in America for promoting research in parapsychology (*psychical research* is the older term), has occasional lectures in New York City. Publishes the *Journal of the American Society for Psychical Research*.

Website: *www.aspr.com*

University of Virginia Division of Perceptual Studies: Carrying on the work of the late Dr. Ian Stevenson. The leading scientific research center for topics like reincarnation, out-of-body experiences, Near-death experiences, and other aspects of parapsychology.

Website: *www.healthsystem.virginia.edu/internet/personalitystudies*

Exceptional Human Experience: The Exceptional Human Experience project studies the personal and transformative meaning at the core of all types of anomalous experiences (335 to date on the Website): mystical, encounter, psychical, healing, death-related, peak, healing, desolation/nadir, and exceptional human performance. The project is especially interested in their aftereffects, the most common being a sense of the connectedness of all things. They have developed an EHE autobiography technique to help potentiate this and other core realizations such as reverence for all life and a sense of planetary stewardship.

Website: *www.ehe.org*

Society for Scientific Exploration: The Society's journal is one of the essential scientific journals to read if you want to keep up with the latest developments in parapsychology and other areas in science that might be "fringe" or the next "cutting edge."

Website: *www.scientificexploration.org*

WEBSITES

GhostVillage: The premier resource for those interested in all things paranormal. Founded and maintained by author and ghost researcher Jeff Belanger. Also provides contact information for amateur paranormal investigators around the nation. (*www.ghostvillage.com*)

Dead Conversations blog: Compelling blog detailing the extraordinary, everyday life of a Canadian medium. (*www.dedcon.blogspot.com*)

Angel's Ghosts: Ever-expanding treasure trove of personal accounts and photographs of ghostly encounters, angelic and demonic visitations, and more. (*www.angelsghosts.com*)

True Ghost Tales: David Slone's fascinating collection of true stories of the paranormal, as contributed by readers. (*www.trueghosttales.com*)

Prairie Ghosts: Largely historical, established archive created and maintained by prolific author and ghost researcher Troy Taylor. (*www.prairieghosts.com*)

Autism and Spirituality: Author William Stillman's Website. (*www.williamstillman.com*)

Children's Past Lives: Well-known past life researcher's Website for the Carol Bowman Past Life Center. (*www.childpastlives.org*)

Indigo Children: Website dedicated to raising the awareness and understanding of so-called Indigo and other special children. (*www.indigochild.com*)

Ouija Boards: History and mystery of the always-fascinating "mystifying oracle." (*www.museumoftalkingboards.com*)

BIBLIOGRAPHY AND SUGGESTED READING

Allen, Thomas B. *Possessed: The True Story of An Exorcism.* 1st ed. New York: Doubleday, 1993.

Auerbach, Loyd. *Ghost Hunting: How to Investigate the Paranormal.* Berkeley, Calif.: Ronin Publishing, 2003.

Becker, Helaine. *Are You Psychic?: The Official Guide for Kids.* Toronto, Ontario: Maple Tree Press, 2005.

Belanger, Jeff. *Communicating With the Dead.* Franklin Lakes, N.J.: New Page Books, 2004.

Benson, Robert Hugh. *Lourdes (Illustrated Edition).* New York: Dodo Press, 2007.

Bertone, Cardinal Tarcisio. *The Last Secret of Fatima.* New York: Doubleday Religion, 2008.

Bord, Janet. A Traveller's Guide to Fairy Sites. Gothic Glastonbury, UK: Gothic Image Publications, 2004.

Browning, Robert. *The Pied Piper of Hamelin, Illustrated by Hope Dunlap.* New York: Yesterday's Classics, 2008.

Bruce, Robert. *Practical Psychic Self-Defense: Understanding and Surviving Unseen Influences.* Charlottesville. Va: Hampton Roads Publishing Company, 2002.

Brunvand, Jan Harold. *The Study of American Folklore: An Introduction (4th Edition).* New York: W.W. Norton & Company, 1998.

———. *The Vanishing Hitchhiker: American Urban Legends and Their Meanings.* New York: W.W. Norton & Company, 1989.

Burns, Patrick, Marley Gibson, and Dave Schrader. *Ghost Hunting: The Ins and Outs of Paranormal Investigations.* United States: Graphia, 2009.

Carroll, Lee, and Jan Tober. *The Indigo Children: The New Kids Have Arrived.* 1st ed. Carlsbad, Calif.: Hay House, 1999.

Carus, Louise. *The Real St. Nicholas: Tales of Generosity and Hope From Around the World.* 1st ed. Wheaton, Ill.: Quest Books, 2002.

Chase, Robert David, Ed Warren, and Lorraine Warren. *Ghost Hunters: True Stories from the World's Most Famous Demonologists.* 1st ed. New York: St .Martins Press, 1989.

Connell, Janice T.. *The Visions of the Children: The Apparitions of the Blessed Mother at Medjugorje: All the Messages of the Blessed Mother and the Latest Unfolding of God's Plan for the Human Race from Medjugorge.* Revised and Updated ed. New York: St. Martin's Griffin, 2007.

Cooper, Joe. *Case of the Cottingley Fairies.* New York: Firebird Distributing, 1998.

Curran, Bob. *A Field Guide to Irish Fairies.* San Francisco, Calif.: Chronicle Books, 1998.

Doyle, Arthur Conan. *Coming of the Fairies.* York Beach: Samuel Weiser, 1972.

Fiore, Edith. *The Unquiet Dead: A Psychologist Treats Spirit Possession.* Chicago: Ballantine Books, 1995.

Gallagher, Lynne. *Psychic Kids.* Cork: Mercier Press, 2008.

Goode, Caron B. *Kids Who See Ghosts: How to Guide Them Through Fear.* San Francisco, Calif.: Weiser Books, 2010.

Hanson, Georg. *The Trickster and the Paranormal.* Bloomington, Ind.: Xlibris Corporation, 2001.

Hunt, Stoker. *Ouija: The Most Dangerous Game.* Brattleboro: Harper Paperbacks, 1992.

Lecuyer, Judith. *Mommy! Ben Made the Cake Fly!": Autistic Children and Paranormal Communication*. Bangor, Maine: *Booklocker.com*, 2001.

Leininger, Andrea, and Bruce Leininger. *Soul Survivor: The Reincarnation of a World War II Fighter Pilot*. New York: Grand Central Publishing, 2009.

Losey, Meg Blackburn. *The Children of Now: Crystalline Children, Indigo Children, Star Kids, Angels on Earth, and the Phenomenon of Transitional Children*. Franklin Lakes, N.J.: New Page Books, 2006.

Mills, Carol Howell, and Tag Powell. *ESP for Kids: How to Develop Your Child's Psychic Ability*. Whitefish: Top of the Mountain Publishing, 1993.

Newcomb, Jacky. *Angel Kids: Enchanting Stories of True-Life Guardian Angels and "Sixth Sense" Abilties in Children*. Carlsbad, Calif.: Hay House, 2009.

Paquette, Ammi-Joan. *The Tiptoe Guide to Tracking Fairies*. Terre Haute, Ind.: Tanglewood Press, 2009.

Roll, William, and Valerie Storey. *Unleashed: Of Poltergeists and Murder: The Curious Story of Tina Resch*. New York/London/Toronto/Sydney: Paraview Pocket Books, 2004.

Roll, William G. *The Poltergeist*. Special ed. New York: Paraview Special Editions, 2004.

Sawyer, J F. *Deliver Us From Evil: True Cases of Haunted Houses and Demonic Attacks: Taken from the files of Ed and Lorraine Warren Demonologist and Medium*. New York: Omnimedia LLC, 2009.

Shroder, Thomas. *Old Souls: Compelling Evidence from Children Who Remember Past Lives*. *1st Fireside ed*. New York: Simon & Schuster, 2001.

Stern, Marina T. *To Live With the Fairy Folk: A Guide to Attract Benevolent Spirits*. York Beach, Maine: Red Wheel/ Weiser, 2002.

Stevenson, Ian. *Children Who Remember Previous Lives: A Question of Reincarnation*. *Revised ed*. Jefferson, N.C.: Mcfarland & Company, 2000.

————. *Twenty Cases Suggestive of Reincarnation: Second Edition, Revised and Enlarged*. *Rev. ed*. Charlottesville, Va.: University Of Virginia Press, 1980.

Stevenson, M.D., Ian. *European Cases of the Reincarnation Type*. North Carolina. Mcfarland, 2008.

Stillman, William. *Autism and the God Connection*. Naperville, Ill.: Sourcebooks, Inc., 2006.

Tucker, Jim. *Life Before Life: Children's Memories of Previous Lives*. *1st ed*. New York: St. Martin's Griffin, 2008.

Virtue, Doreen. *The Care and Feeding of Indigo Children*. Carlsbad, Calif.: Hay House, 2001.

Warren, Joshua P. *Pet Ghosts: Animal Encounters from Beyond the Grave*. *1st ed*. Franklin Lakes, N.J.: New Page Books, 2006.

Weisberg, Barbara. *Talking to the Dead: Kate and Maggie Fox and the Rise of Spiritualism*. New York: HarperOne, 2005.

INDEX

ABOUT THE AUTHOR

Ursula Bielski is the founder of Chicago Hauntings, Inc. A historian, author, and parapsychology enthusiast, she has been writing and lecturing about Chicago's supernatural folklore and the paranormal for more than 20 years, and is recognized as a leading authority on the Chicago region's ghostlore and cemetery history. She is the author of five popular and critically acclaimed books on the same subjects.

Ursula's interests in Chicago ghost hunting began at a young age. She grew up in a haunted house on Chicago's north side and received an early education in Chicago history from her father, a Chicago police officer, who introduced Ursula to the ghosts at Graceland Cemetery, Montrose Point ,and the old lockup at the storied Maxwell Street Police Station. Since that time Ursula has been involved in countless investigations of haunted sites in and around Chicago, including such notorious locales as Wrigley Field, the Congress Hotel, the Indiana Dunes, the Red Lion Pub, Hull House, Bachelors Grove Cemetery, Rose Hill Cemetery, haunted Archer Avenue, Chinatown, the Eastland disaster site, Death Alley, Dillinger's Alley, and the St. Valentine's Day Massacre site. Her paranormal travels have also led her to investigate sites as diverse and infamous as the Bell Witch Cave in Tennessee; the Oshkosh, Wisconsin, Opera House; New Orleans' House of the Rising Sun; the City Cemetery in Key West, Florida; and the Civil War Battlefield at Gettysburg, Pennsylvania.

Aside from her writing, Ursula has been featured on numerous television documentaries, including productions by the A&E Network, The History Channel, The Learning Channel, The Travel Channel, and PBS. She also appears regularly on local Chicago television and radio and lectures throughout the year at various libraries, and historical and professional societies. In addition to her books, Ursula is the author of numerous scholarly articles exploring the links between history and the paranormal, including articles published in the *International Journal of Parapsychology*. Ursula is a past editor of *PA News*, the quarterly newsletter of the Parapsychological Association, is a past president and board member of the Pi Gamma Chapter of Phi Alpha Theta, the national history honor society, and holds membership in the Society of Midland Authors.

A graduate of St. Benedict High School in Chicago, Ursula holds a BA in history from Benedictine University and an MA in American cultural and intellectual history from Northeastern Illinois University. Her academic explorations include the Spiritualist movement of the 19th century and its transformation into psychical research and parapsychology, and the relationships among belief, experience, science, and religion.

She lives in Chicago with her two daughters.